EPHESIANS

Upward Faith

AN EIGHT-WEEK STUDY WITH

Dr. Tony W. Cartledge

THE *Nurturing*
FAITH™
BIBLE STUDY SERIES

© 2015

Published in the United States by Nurturing Faith Inc., Macon GA,
www.nurturingfaith.net.

Library of Congress Cataloging-in-Publication Data is available.

ISBN 978-1-938514-90-6

*Unless otherwise indicated, scripture quotations are taken from
the New Revised Version of the Bible.*

Cover photo by Tony W. Cartledge
The restored façade of the library of Celsus in Ephesus.
Interior and cover design by Amy C. Cook

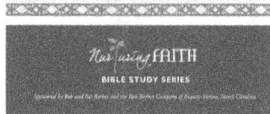

Other resources from

Nurturing Faith
BOOKS

J.K. Wylie

Carole Boseman Taylor

Jon R. Roebuck

Dennis R. Atwood

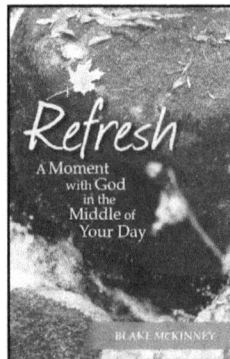

Blake McKinney

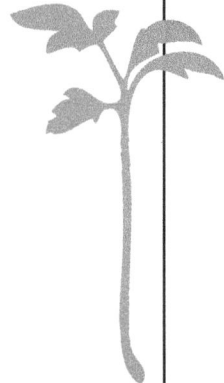

CONTENTS

ABBREVIATIONS

ESV   English Standard Version

KJV   King James Version

HCSB   Holman Christian Standard Bible

NET   New English Translation (also known as the NETBible)

LXX   Septuagint, an early Greek translation of the Old Testament

MT   Masoretic Text, the "standard" Hebrew text of the Old Testament

NASB   New American Standard Bible, 1977 edition

NAS95   New American Standard Bible, 1995 edition

NIV   New International Version, 1984 edition

NIV11   New International Version, 2011 edition

NRSV   New Revised Standard Version

PREFACE

Bible study is a discipline that calls for the engagement of both hearts and minds. The Nurturing Faith Bible Series is designed to focus attention on biblical texts that expand the mind and enrich the heart.

Dr. Tony Cartledge brings the insights of a scholar, the heart of a pastor, and the communication skills of a seasoned writer and editor to this important task. With careful scholarship he guides learners to a clearer understanding of the context—language, culture, and setting—in which the biblical accounts occurred.

Then the important question is considered: "How do these ancient words speak to us as people of faith today?" Truth—not bound by time and culture—awaits those who are willing to dig, contemplate, and apply these biblical treasures.

Respecting the need to engage scripture with both heart and mind, there is no attempt to "dumb down" the lessons or to ignore the challenges of serious inquiry. This is a distinguishing mark of the Nurturing Faith Bible Study Series.

Therefore, each lesson concludes with "The Hardest Question" in which Dr. Cartledge both raises and responds to such challenges in understanding and applying the biblical revelation to today's living.

An honest wrangling with the biblical revelation—while guided by God's Spirit—can produce clearer understanding and stronger commitments. Such Bible study will indeed nurture one's faith.

The lessons in this book explore the instructive writings to early Christians in Ephesus, then a bustling seaport city under Roman rule. Those who study these texts along with Dr. Cartledge will be encouraged to live faithfully in community with other believers and be reminded of how all things are brought together in Christ.

May these eight sessions of studying Ephesians bring new insight into a unique setting of early Christianity and a refreshed experience of commitment to living faithfully today as followers of Christ.

—*John D. Pierce, Publisher*
Nurturing Faith, Inc.

This volume in the Nurturing Faith Bible Study Series
is made possible through a generous gift from
Gene and Linda Pleasants of Raleigh, North Carolina

***

Nurturing Faith seeks sponsors for future volumes in this Bible study series.
To inquire, please contact office@nurturingfaith.net.

INTRODUCTION

EPHESUS AND THE EPHESIANS

Ephesus was an important port city in the first century, located on the west coast of what was then called "Asia," now the country of Turkey. Impressive ruins of the ancient city are located near the modern city of Selçuk and a 45-minute ride from the port of Kusidasi, from which busloads of cruise ship passengers come to admire what remains of its imposing public buildings, temples to various gods, ritzy "terrace houses" occupied by the rich, and public facilities that all could enjoy.

A modern visitor would be puzzled to hear that Ephesus was once a major port, for it sits several miles inland. In the first century, the Cayster River brought a procession of ships to an accessible and protected harbor, but the river silted in long before modern dredging equipment was available. The loss of the harbor contributed significantly to the city's demise.

During its heyday Ephesus was a major city, perhaps second in importance only to Rome. Estimates of its population have exceeded 200,000, though 50,000 is a more reasonable figure. A large theater near the port could seat more than 25,000. The city had a rich history as a Greek and later Roman city. Like most port cities, it was quite cosmopolitan in nature.

Ephesus served as the capital of Asia under Roman rule and was famed as the home of a large temple to the Greek goddess Artemis, known to the Romans as Diana: Acts 19 describes how artisans who sold images of Artemis felt threatened by the Apostle Paul and sparked a riot designed to force him from the city. Today, only a single column remains from that temple.

The Apostle Paul has been traditionally considered to have written the letter to the Ephesians, which begins with the words "Paul, an apostle of Christ Jesus by the will of God, to the saints who are in Ephesus and are faithful in Christ Jesus" (1:1). In it, he describes himself as a "prisoner for Christ Jesus" (3:1) or a "prisoner in the Lord" (4:1), suggesting that he was writing from prison after being arrested for his activities related to spreading the gospel.

Paul was imprisoned briefly on several occasions (2 Cor. 11:23), and after being arrested in Jerusalem (Acts 21:27-36), he was held for trial in the coastal city of Caesarea (about 58-60 C.E., Acts 23-26) before appealing to the emperor and being taken to Rome, where he remained in prison for at least two years and may have been executed there (60-62 C.E., Acts 27-28).

Four of Paul's letters are known as "prison epistles," and include references to his captivity. These include Philippians (1:7, 13-14), Colossians (4:3, 10, 18), Ephesians (3:1, 4:1, 6:20), and Philemon (1, 9, 10, 13, 23). Second Timothy, more commonly regarded as a "pastoral epistle," also claims a prison setting (1:8, 16; 2:8).

Paul had worked among the Ephesians for quite a while (Acts 19), so it is surprising that the letter contains very few personal references, and the author speaks more of having heard about the Ephesians (1:15) than of having known them personally. This has led some scholars to suggest that the actual author was not Paul, but one of his companions or admirers. Thomas B. Slater calls the letter "deutero-Pauline," and Andrew T. Lincoln is even more convinced that a disciple of Paul wrote the letter in Paul's name, drawing heavily on Paul's earlier letter to the Colossians for his imagery.

Other writers maintain that Paul was indeed the author, arguing that the stylistic differences may be due to his use of an *amenuensis* (scribe) who may have flavored Paul's dictation with his own style. The lack of personal references may indicate that Paul was writing mainly for new converts who had come into the church since his time there. For purposes of simplicity, in this book we will refer to the author as Paul while remaining aware that Paul's thought may have been reflected in the words of a close disciple.

The oldest and best Greek manuscripts do not include the words "in Ephesus" (1:1), leading some commentators to believe that the letter was written as an encyclical, to be passed around and read among all the churches, with a blank space in the first sentence to be filled in with the name of each local church.

The first three chapters of Ephesians speak beautifully of how the church fits into God's redeeming plan for the universe, with all things being brought together under Christ (1:9-10). Chapter 3 ends with a prayer and a doxology, as if it were the closing part of the letter.

The last three chapters consist of practical advice and encouragement for readers to live in a way that is worthy of membership in the body of Christ, suggesting that the letter may have come from two hands, or that it may be a composite of two letters. Here's one way of looking at how the letter is organized:

OUTLINE

I. Opening words
   Salutation (1:1-2)
   Blessing (1:3-14)
   Thanksgiving (1:15-23)

II. God's New People
   God's grace in Christ (2:1-10)
   God's people brought near (2:11-22)

III. God's Mystery and Majesty
   The mystery revealed (3:1-13)
   The mystery indwelling Spirit (3:14-21)

IV. God's People in Community
   Living in community (4:1-16)
   Living as God's people (4:17-5:2)
   Maintaining community (5:3-20)

V. God's People at Home
   Husbands and wives (5:21-33)
   Parents and children (6:1-4)
   Masters and servants (6:5-9)

VI. Concluding Remarks
   The army of God (6:10-17)
   Prayer requests and blessings (6:18-24)

In preparing these lessons, I became aware that the gist of several of them could be expressed in a brief phrase using the word "up." While it may seem artificial, chapter titles for this book follow that theme, considering ways we may look up to God, grow up in Christ, and build up the church. The lessons included here do not cover every verse in Ephesians, including the frequently debated "house rules" of 5:21–6:9, which are often studied in other settings. Still these lessons touch on all of the most important themes and challenges of this inspiring and instructive epistle.

RESOURCES

Bruce, F. F. *The Epistles to the Colossians, to Philemon, and to the Ephesians.* New International
 Commentary on the New Testament. Grand Rapids: Eerdmanns, 1984.

Lincoln, Andrew T. *Ephesians.* Word Biblical Commentary. Waco: Word Books, 1990.

Martin, Ralph. "Ephesians," in *The Broadman Bible Commentary*, vol. 11. Nashville:
 Broadman Press, 1971.

Nash, Scott, ed. *Interpreting Ephesians for Preaching and Teaching.* Macon, GA: Smyth &
 Helwys, 1996.

Slater, Thomas B. *Ephesians.* Smyth & Helwys Bible Commentary. Macon, GA: Smyth &
 Helwys, 2012.

Stagg, Frank. "Ephesians," in the *Mercer Commentary on the Bible*. Macon, GA: Mercer
 University Press, 1995.

Tolbert, Malcolm. *Ephesians: God's New People.* Nashville: Convention Press, 1979.

Ephesians 1:3-14

LOOK UP!

In him we have redemption through his blood,
the forgiveness of our trespasses,
according to the riches of his grace that he lavished on us.
—Ephesians 1:7-8a

Have you ever inherited something? Getting through the legal complexities of actually obtaining an inheritance can be challenging for executors and beneficiaries alike, but when all is said and done, the estates left by others can become a real blessing to the deceased person's descendants, friends, or chosen charities.

Receiving an inheritance can be a blessing in the present, but also a tie to the past. With my two brothers, I own a third of a 17-acre property that my father has already put in our names. He inherited it from his mother, and she from my great-grandmother. It gives me joy to walk past the tumble-down house and barn built from timber milled on site, then to stroll through the pasture and into the piney woods behind a small pond. Knowing that it comes to me as a family inheritance makes it special.

Ephesians 1 speaks of an incomparable inheritance that comes, not from any earthly source, but from God.

IN CHRIST WE ARE BLESSED
(vv. 3-6)

Ephesians 1:3-14 is astonishing in its grammatical complexity. In the Greek text, the entire passage is written as one sentence—one long, breathless, eye-popping call for Christian people to look up to God and fill their lives with days of praise for all that God has done. Fortunately, English translations tend to break the complex construction into more digestible bits.

Paul begins with a reminder of the many ways God has blessed us, careful to point out that these blessings come through Jesus Christ. Throughout this text, "in him" and "in Christ" serve as key words. We have these blessings—blessings that have changed our lives and can change others through us—through the one we call Jesus, the Christ.

Paul rejoices that God has blessed us in Christ with "every spiritual blessing" (v. 3), and the first of these is that God has chosen us to be adopted as children through the work of Christ (vv. 4-6). Traditions that hold to a belief in predestination depend heavily on this text, interpreting it to suggest that God has chosen certain persons to be saved, even before the foundation of the world.

The problem with a strong view of personal predestination is that it robs humankind of any kind of meaningful freedom while also undermining the missionary imperative of the gospel. That mission mandate is taught far more clearly than the few ambiguous references used to support a belief in predestination.

If God has already chosen every person who will be saved, then one could argue that there is no point in spreading the gospel, because God will save whom God desires with no help from us. In the early part of the mid-19th century, Baptists engaged in a heated conflict between "Particular Baptists," who believed that Christ died only for those particular "elect" persons, and "General Baptists," who believed that Christ died for all. The missionary versus anti-missionary controversy split many churches, sometimes resulting in side-by-side "Missionary" and "Primitive" (anti-missionary) Baptist churches. ⬇ ⬇

Some non-predestinarians deal with the troublesome text by affirming that God simply knows who will accept Christ even before they do, but there is another way to read the text. The point Paul is making is not that God has foreordained Simon and Sally to be saved and adopted as God's

---

⬇ **Good seed, or bad?**

In America, a prime mover in the predestinarian-inspired anti-mission movement was a preacher named Daniel Parker. In an 1826 pamphlet titled "Views on the Two Seeds," he taught that every person possesses either a "good seed" of godliness (equivalent to "the elect" of Calvinist teaching) or a "bad seed" of the devil (equivalent to the "non-elect"). Some early churches came to be known as "Two Seed in the Spirit Baptists," while others were described with terms such as "Old School," "Predestinarian," or "Primitive."

> ⚓ **Missionary, or no?** Today's "Primitive Baptist" churches, descendents of the fervently Calvinistic anti-missionary movement, tend to be very small, and many have died out altogether. While mission-minded churches are also subject to decline for a variety of reasons, they are much less likely to diminish and go out of business than their anti-mission cousins. Can you point to the very logical reason why this is so?

children, while rejecting Mabel and Matthew. Remember that Paul is writing *to the church*—to a group of people who have chosen to follow Christ. God has in fact fore-ordained that every person who trusts in Christ can be saved, can become a part of the church, can experience all the blessings that God wants his children to have.

God saves us not only as individuals, but also as a community of faith. Paul is not teaching that God's eternal plan has a roster of predestined believers, but that God's eternal providence has a place for every person who chooses to accept the gift of divine grace. Those who believe this cannot help but give praise to God.

IN CHRIST WE HAVE REDEMPTION
(vv. 7-10)

After Paul introduces his theme in vv. 3-6, he begins three of the remaining sections of this lengthy 12-verse sentence with the words "in him." Some translations substitute the word "Christ" for "him" as a means for clarifying that the pronoun always refers back to Christ.

In vv. 7-10, Paul affirms that in Christ we have redemption. We have forgiveness. We have access to an amazing grace that is beyond our comprehension. We are all guilty of sin, guilty of rebellion against God's way, guilty of living for self with little thought for others. At some point, most of us have been guilty of lying, cheating, lusting, and worse.

And yet Paul says, "In him we have redemption through his blood, the forgiveness of our trespasses, according to the riches of his grace that he lavished on us" (vv. 7-8a). We could never fully pay for our sins—if God had a prison for sinners, we would all be inmates for the rest of our lives—but Christ has declared us forgiven. In some marvelous way far beyond our comprehension, we can experience redemption through his blood—the forgiveness of our sins.

The word Paul uses for "forgiveness" (*aphesis*) is the technical Greek term that refers to a legal pardon. It is a mystery to us that God would love us so, and take pleasure in redeeming us. It's no wonder that Paul would celebrate it.

> **For Reflection:** *What are some common and creative ways we can thank God for the amazing grace that makes possible our redemption?*

IN CHRIST WE HAVE AN INHERITANCE
(vv. 11-12)

Paul goes on to make the remarkable claim that God not only loves us enough to save us and adopt us as children, but also that God has set aside a surprising inheritance for those who set their hope in Christ: that we "might live for the praise of his glory" (vv. 11-12).

Paul grew up in a Jewish family. He would have grown up hearing or reading about the inheritance of the land that God had promised to Israel. In the gospel he had learned of an even greater inheritance, an eternal one, offered to those who trust in God. This inheritance doesn't come when someone else dies, in the normal order of events. The inheritance is ours even now, but we experience it in full when we die. ⸙

Paul makes a point of saying that this is one reason God has planned such

⸙**A heavenly hope:** Back in the 1990s, not long after my young daughter Bethany had been killed in a car crash caused by a drunk driver, I accompanied a church mission team to Williamsburg, Kentucky. We spent most of the week doing a variety of construction and repair jobs on the decrepit homes of impoverished families, but one evening we took a break to visit Cumberland Falls.

The Cumberland River runs quietly through mountain valleys until it gets to just that spot, where it turns to thunder as it pours in a horseshoe-shaped cataract some 68 feet high and 125 feet wide. A heavy mist rises from the foot of the falls, watering plants that cling to life on bare rock across both sides of the valley. On clear nights, when the moon is bright, a "moonbow" can be seen in the rising mist. It is an impressive, heart-pounding sight. As I stood and looked over the roaring falls, I thought, "I wish I could show this to Bethany."

Then it occurred to me, "If only a fraction of what we believe about heaven is true, then Bethany has far more wonderful things than this to show me!" In Christ we have the hope of an eternal inheritance that gives us daily cause for praise and for joy.

a glorious future for us—that we might be motivated to live in praise to God: "so that we, who were the first to set our hope on Christ, might live for the praise of his glory" (v. 12).

Paul believed the first generation of Christian believers had a notable privilege and a special responsibility. Their lives of praise would set a pattern for others to follow as they called them to lives of faith. We are called to follow in the pattern and witness to others through our own grateful living.

If you've ever helped to put shingles on a house, you learned that every row of shingles is a guide for those that come after. The man who first instructed me in the art of roofing also cut a piece of scrap shingle to the proper length so I could use it to check that each succeeding row was just the right distance above the one below: he called the handy guide a "preacher."

In a similar fashion, every generation of Christians provides a pattern for the next to follow, and sometimes we need a good preacher to keep us straight. If we would lead those who come after us rightly, then we will lead them to offer praise to God, not just with their words, but with their actions.

We don't just praise God when we sing hymns on Sunday, but when we show love to a child on Monday, when we feed the hungry on Tuesday, when we listen to a hurting friend on Wednesday. We praise God with our lives when we visit the sick on Thursday, when we repair a toilet on Friday, even when we enjoy wholesome family recreation on Saturday. Because Jesus Christ has filled our hearts with amazing grace, we fill our lives with days of praise.

> **For Reflection:** *Think of practical ways you can show praise to God through service, as well as worship. Consider this: In Hebrew, the same word is used to mean both "service" and "worship"—and we typically speak of a "worship service." What are some ways we can express our worship of God through service to others?*

IN CHRIST WE KNOW THE HOLY SPIRIT
(vv. 13-14)

All of this sounds good, but we know that there are days when we don't feel so full of praise, and we may question how real this eternal inheritance might be. Paul's response was to insist that God offers a taste of heaven on earth as we open our hearts and lives to the presence of the Holy Spirit that marks us like an indelible seal. The Spirit is the "pledge of our inheritance toward redemption as God's own people," Paul said, "to the praise of his glory" (vv. 13-14).

Jesus no longer walks with us as he walked with Mary and Martha and Peter and John. Even in Paul's day, Jesus was no longer present in that physical way. But Paul believed Christ's promise to be present through the Spirit. Paul had experienced the touch of God's Spirit, and believed that the Spirit's touch today is the guarantee of God's embrace tomorrow.

The Spirit of Christ in our lives works not only as an internal guide to direct our living, but also as an outward mark of our redemption because of the change the Spirit works in our lives.

In Jesus Christ we have redemption from our sins. We have an inheritance in eternity. We have a present comforter and guide. We have, in short, all that we need for a life that is filled with meaning and laced with praise.

> **For Reflection:** *Paul encourages believers to look up and reflect on God's many blessings, thanking God for the promise of Christ's presence through the Spirit of God. Think of practical ways you can take time to "look up" and be grateful every day.*

THE HARDEST QUESTION

What about predestination?

The past 20 years have seen a sharp resurgence in Calvinism, even within denominations long known for their missionary focus. The "Calvinist" label comes from John Calvin, a 16th-century French theologian who was among the second generation of leaders of the Protestant Reformation. Calvin strongly emphasized the absolute sovereignty of God in matters of salvation, a teaching that God has predestined who will be saved and who will not.

Though some modern Calvinists prefer different terminology, the central beliefs of classic Calvinism are traditionally described by the acronym "TULIP." They are:

Total depravity: All humans are so tainted by sin that they are not capable of responding to God on their own.

Unconditional election: God has foreordained who will be saved and who will be condemned; humans have no choice in the matter.

Limited atonement: Christ's death provided atonement for sin, but only for those "elect" whom God has designated for salvation.

Irresistible grace: When God calls the elect through the Holy Spirit, they are incapable of resisting the gospel.

Perseverance of the saints: Those whom God has elected to salvation will persevere and not turn away from their faith.

A few biblical references can be cited that seem to support a belief in pre-destination, including one from the first chapter of Ephesians, which speaks of those who have been "destined according to the purpose of him who accomplishes all things according to his counsel and will" (1:8). Romans 8:29-30 expresses similar sentiments. Other verses, such as John 6:44, are sometimes cited: "No one can come to me unless drawn by the Father who sent me." But none of those verses rules out the possibility that God's call and desire for human salvation extends to all persons, not just a select group of "elect."

While a few texts may be cited in support of limited atonement, many others are clear calls for all people to respond to Christ, not just "the elect." We are familiar with John 3:16, for example: "For God so loved the world that he gave his only Son, so that everyone who believes in him may not perish but may have eternal life." Jesus' teachings do not suggest that only certain people are allowed to believe, but "whosoever," as the KJV puts it. The next verse makes it even clearer that the gospel is for the entire world: "Indeed, God did not send the Son into the world to condemn the world, but in order that the world might be saved through him." Many other texts could be cited. Think, for example, of Jesus' "great commission" of Matt. 28:19-20, or Acts 1:8. Christ sends us to every nation, "to the ends of the earth." Nothing about that calling suggests that anyone is excluded from hearing and responding to the gospel.

Ephesians 2:1-10

RISE UP!

For by grace you have been saved through faith,
and this is not your own doing; it is the gift of God—
not the result of works, so that no one may boast.
—Ephesians 2:8-9

Have you ever been frustrated, wishing your life had a greater sense of purpose? That's not uncommon: Surely we all want to believe our lives have some meaning beyond self-gratification. Many people take an active approach to seeking (or making) a place of significance in the world. They may pursue higher education, influential jobs, or activities they believe will make a difference.

Others want to believe life has a purpose, but take a less active—and more fatalistic—approach. They seem to assume that whatever happens to them is a part of God's plan, though they may make no apparent effort to live godly lives. No matter what happens, even when tragedy strikes, they calmly recite a common but questionable mantra of folk religion: "I believe everything happens for a purpose."

The hunger for greater purpose in life has contributed to the popularity of mega-church pastor Rick Warren's *The Purpose Driven Life* (Grand Rapids: Zondervan, 2002), which continues to set sales records long after its release, and has spawned an avalanche of related products. Since Warren first introduced the program at Saddleback Valley Community Church, hundreds of congregations have participated in a formulaic "Forty Days of Purpose" emphasis.

Why the excitement? Because the subject matter taps into a deep human need: We want to believe there is meaning to life, that we have a purpose bigger than living from one day to the next. Even though Warren's book insists

"It's not about you," the longing to find purpose in life is very much about us. We want to know that our lives matter, that we have some role to play in God's world.

In Eph. 2:1-10, the Apostle Paul speaks of what it is like to be human, to be lost, to be in need of salvation. He tells us that God has made salvation possible through our expression of faith in Christ. And, he tells us that God has created and saved us for a purpose: that we might do good works. *Saved to do good works?* That is a surprising and often overlooked twist at the end of an exhortation more commonly remembered for its emphasis on salvation by faith rather than works.

HUMAN HOPELESSNESS
(vv. 1-3)

Paul's letter to the Ephesians is a missive of encouragement to beloved friends in the faith, most of whom were Gentiles. In Eph. 2:1-10, Paul reminds Gentile believers of the importance of God's grace and God's way of life. He wants his friends to understand where they have come from in their relationship to God, where they are in the present, and where they are going.

Some of what Paul shared with the Ephesians seemed strange and new. Paul believed that Christian people were called to worship and work together despite their different ethnic backgrounds and life experiences. He knew that regardless of our income level or color or gender or occupation, we all have the same spiritual needs. Paul believed those needs could be met only through Christ, and he spoke of people who did not know Christ as spiritually "dead."

In this chapter, Paul speaks mainly to Gentiles, to people who were not born Jewish. That would include the vast majority of those who are reading this book. Paul tells us where we have come from: "You were dead through the trespasses and sins in which you once lived" (v. 1). "Trespasses" and "sins" are virtual synonyms. The Greek term for "trespasses" means "to go out of bounds," and the word translated as "sins" means "to miss the target." Without Christ we are spiritually dead because we have chosen a life that alienates us from God. We have missed the way of fellowship with God because we have gone out of bounds in pursuit of "the course of this world" (v. 2a).

Paul wrote so that people could understand him, including his use of a popular concept that those who adopted the way of the world were following an evil power at work in the world. Paul described the evil power as "the ruler of the power of the air, the spirit that is now at work among those who are disobedient" (v. 2b). 🔖

⬇ **Air pollution:** Ancient Greeks believed that the earth was flat and covered by a huge dome. Inside this dome, near the ground, was a lower layer of polluted air called the *aeros*, which gave way to a higher layer of clean air called the *ether*. People commonly thought that the layer of impure air closest to the earth was the abode of wicked spirits and demons, who were organized under the rule of a "prince of the power of the air," the chief evil spirit.

Some interpreters would identify this notion of a wicked and powerful spirit with Satan, "the spirit that is now at work among those who are disobedient." The salvation event in Christ Jesus will ultimately overcome all evil, but in the meantime, the power of evil is still very evident in our world.

In v. 3, Paul makes it clear that this hopeless condition was not unique to the Gentiles. The Jews, too, had given themselves over to "passions of our flesh, following the desires of flesh and senses," so that they were "by nature children of wrath, like everyone else." Being born Jewish does not put one right with God, any more than being baptized as an infant or added to the "cradle roll" of a church before birth. Beginning life within a religious tradition gives us many opportunities to become people of faith, but developing a personal commitment to God is just that—personal.

The words for "passions" or "desires" can have either good or bad connotations. Having passions and desires is not wrong; what matters is the direction of those passions. Here, the context makes it decidedly negative. Paul insists that we cannot blame our evil desires and our sinful actions on any external force, however: They are "of flesh and senses"—that is, of the body and of the mind. Our sins are the result of our own desires and choices. As a result, unregenerate Jews and Gentiles alike are "by nature children of wrath." As such, we tend to live in selfish ways that are counter to God's purpose for us and for the world.

DIVINE HELP
(vv. 4-7)

We may be grateful that Paul did not stop writing after v. 3. We came from a place of sin and death, but can rejoice that God has opened the door so we can rise up to experience a most meaningful life. "But God, who is rich in mercy, out of the great love with which he loved us even when we were dead through our trespasses, made us alive together with Christ—by grace you have been saved" (vv. 4-5). ⬇

God's love and mercy are more powerful than sin and death. That is good

Rise! In other places, Paul also speaks of believers as having been dead but raised in Christ. Later in Ephesians he quotes an earlier writing or saying: "Sleeper, awake! Rise from the dead, and Christ will shine on you."

news, because we have the power to lose ourselves, but we cannot save ourselves. Left to our own nature, we commit spiritual suicide, but because of his love, God through Christ has cleared a path for us to find new life.

We must not overlook an important word: *together*. "God made us alive *together* with Christ." God did not save us in order to make us "Lone Ranger" Christians. God did not intend for us to sit isolated in our houses, pray only in our prayer closets, or care for ourselves alone. God has "raised us up with him" to participate in the eternal kingdom (vv. 6-7), and God's kingdom involves community.

Long before it became popular to self-identify as "spiritual but not religious," the late Malcolm Tolbert stressed the importance of community: "Individual redemption has meaning only as it is a part of God's total redemptive work in creating the people of God. For a person to be converted and at the same time deny what God has done in the lives of fellow believers is an abortion and not a birth. Birth brings people into the family. Conversion brings one into God's family, God's new people."[1]

Recognizing our place in a larger family reminds us that we have responsibilities based on our connection to a larger world. We come into this relationship through the work of God's grace, and we come to realize that the same grace will put us to work.

For Reflection: *Perhaps you have spent time in church, and time out of church. What role does the fellowship of other believers play in our spiritual growth and daily expression of faith?*

GRACE WORKS
(vv. 8-10)

Did you ever memorize Eph. 2:8-9? The KJV translation I learned as a child is classic: "For by grace are ye saved through faith; and that not of yourselves; it is the gift of God; not of works, lest any man should boast" (nor any woman or child, for that matter).

There is nothing we can do to save ourselves, but thankfully, that's not our problem. Jesus Christ has already done what needs to be done to rescue us from the way of death and to set us on the road to eternity. With Paul, we can proclaim the incredible belief that Jesus loved us enough to leave the wonders of heaven and come to the earth. He took our humanity upon himself: our sin, our suffering, even the death we deserve. ♆

New Testament writers believed that in Christ's life, death, and resurrection he overcame the power of evil and blazed a path into glory for all those who will choose to follow. He did that for us because we could not do it for ourselves. We call that *grace*. We accept it by *faith*: "by grace you have been saved through faith," Paul writes, "and this is not your own doing: it is the gift of God" (v. 8).

Now Paul shifts gears to address what should happen after we accept God's grace. Paul was always faced with the

♆ **Incarnation:** The belief that Christ left heaven and temporarily surrendered some of his divine qualities is expressed in the theological term "incarnation." The word comes from the Latin verb *incarnere*, which is built from the prefix *in-* and the noun root *carn-* ("flesh"). It literally means "enfleshment," and is commonly used to refer to Christ putting on flesh and becoming fully human in Jesus. Paul expressed the idea of incarnation beautifully in Phil. 2:5-8:

> Let the same mind be in you
> that was in Christ Jesus, who,
> though he was in the form of
> God, did not regard equality
> with God as something to be
> exploited, but emptied himself,
> taking the form of a slave, being
> born in human likeness. And
> being found in human form, he
> humbled himself and became
> obedient to the point of death—
> even death on a cross.

challenge of balancing the concepts of faith and works. He wanted to emphasize the lavish and free grace of God, but he knew that there would always be libertines who would distort God's grace to promote licentious living.

So, he stressed our absolute dependency on God's grace in vv. 8-9: Our salvation is a gift of God, not the result of our own works—no matter how many. This does not mean, however, that what we do is not important. Christians are not saved *by* good works, but they are saved *for* good works.

Paul makes this clear in v. 10, a verse less familiar but brimming with meaning: "For we are what he has made us, created in Christ Jesus for good works, which God prepared beforehand to be our way of life." How amazing it is to ponder the thought that we are what he has made us, in all of our uniqueness. ♆ We don't look the same, and we don't dress the same. We don't act the same, and we don't think the same. There are no two people whose brains work in exactly the same way. We don't find the same things or the same people interesting. We're different!

Some of us have quick tempers, while others have the patience of Job. Some are easily upset, while others have emotions of steel. We're different!

Some of us are neat-niks, and others are sloppy. Some of us munch potato chips in bed, and others won't eat anything outside of the dining room. Some of us snore, some don't. Some of us are early birds, and others are night owls. We're different!

> ♦ **What he has made us:** The more familiar KJV and NIV translations say "we are his workmanship," because the noun used here is derived from a verb meaning "to do," "to make," or "to work." Literally, the noun means "something made." Believers—as individuals and as a church—are made by Christ, and made for a purpose: to do good works. This has always been God's intention for us. Christ sets us free to become redeemed, responsible persons who make the world a better place.

Some of us like things to be black and white, while others are more comfortable with gray shades of ambiguity. Some are comfortable in the modern world where reason rules, while others are happily and mystically postmodern. We're different!

And none of us has any monopoly on being the right way to be. God made us all, and "We are what he has made us," Paul said.

What we have in common is that we all are human, we all are sinners, we all stand in need of divine grace. God calls each of us to have the same faith in the same grace in the same Lord Jesus Christ. As redeemed people, he calls us every one to commit our lives to Christ, to Christ's body, the church, and to Christ's favorite children, the hurting and lonely people of our world. We are unique people, called to rise from spiritual death to live with a common purpose.

Unity in diversity, based on theology, committed to good works that bless the world . . . what a concept!

> **For Reflection:** *Have you ever considered the thought that we are created for a purpose, and that purpose is to do good works in Christ's behalf? What kinds of activities come to mind when you think of "good works"? Can you name things you have done this past week that contribute to making the world a better place?*

THE HARDEST QUESTION

What did God prepare beforehand?

Look again at v. 10: "For we are what he has made us, created in Christ Jesus for good works, which God prepared beforehand to be our way of life."

What is it that God "prepared beforehand": believers who are made to do good works, or the good works themselves?

Through the years, commentators have taken different positions. The relative pronoun used (*hois*) is dative in form, indicating purpose, and a straightforward translation connects "which God prepared beforehand" with "good works," which immediately precedes the phrase. But, some have asked, how could good works exist before they are actually done?

Some have avoided the problem by positing that an implicit "us" should be the object of the verb "prepared beforehand," reading the verse to mean that God prepared believers beforehand so they might do good works.

Others have suggested that "prepared beforehand" refers to the believer's baptism and filling with the spirit, which prepares him or her to do the good works for which God has created us.

Neither of these approaches is necessary. Surely we could speak of values such as love, justice, or beneficence as having their source in God before people manifested them on earth, and the same could be said of good works.

Andrew T. Lincoln concludes his discussion of the question this way: "If believers are God's work, then their ethical activity must also proceed from God and so can be thought of as already prepared in God's counsel. Not just their initial reception of salvation, but the whole of believers' lives, including their practical ethical activity, is to be seen as part of God's purpose. The thought of 2:10 is that the good works were already there, and when, through his grace, God made believers alive, raised them up, and seated them with Christ, he created them for these works."[2]

Recall these words from Paul's opening blessing: "Blessed be the God and Father of our Lord Jesus Christ, who has blessed us in Christ with every spiritual blessing in the heavenly places, just as he chose us in Christ before the foundation of the world to be holy and blameless before him in love" (1:3-4).

Just as God destined from the foundation of the world to offer grace to those who seek God's way, God also had in mind these good works "to be our way of life" (2:10b). And what better way to summarize what it means to do the good works God has prepared than "to be holy and blameless before him in love" (1:4b)? Purity in our relationship to God, gracious charity in relationship to others—that just about covers it.

NOTES

[1]Malcolm Tolbert, *Ephesians: God's New People* (Nashville: Convention Press, 1979), 43.

[2]Andrew T. Lincoln, *Ephesians*, Word Biblical Commentary (Waco: Word Books, 1990), 115.

Ephesians 2:11-22

HUDDLE UP!

So then you are no longer strangers and aliens,
but you are citizens with the saints and also
members of the household of God.
—Ephesians 2:19

Have you ever been in a situation where you were such a complete stranger that you might as well have been a space alien? I first had that experience in 1971, when I served in Indonesia as a summer missionary. I was considerably larger than most Indonesians, my skin was much lighter, my hair was Beatle-length, and I often wore a solid red shirt with bell-bottom pants that had vertical red, white, and blue stripes (remember, it was 1971). Everywhere I went, children would point and talk about me in their lovely musical language. I might as well have been from Beta Centauri.

I also remember feeling like an alien the first time I attended a Lutheran worship service. I didn't know when to stand, when to sit, when to kneel. I didn't know the responsive words to the short litanies that kept popping up. It was not a particularly comfortable experience.

Ephesians 2:11-22 is about what it feels like to be a stranger to the family of God, and about what God has done to bring an end to our alienation from him, and from each other.

ALIENS, AND NOT . . .
(vv. 11-13)

Some scholars assume that Paul wrote Ephesians, while others believe it was written by an admirer who reflected Paul's thought, but the letter claims to have been written by the apostle during a time of imprisonment. If so, he would have been writing as a Jewish Christian leader to a congregation composed mainly of Gentile Christians. That marked a startling shift in the ancient world. Jesus was born as a Jew, and later New Testament writers believed that his ministry filled the role of the longed-for Jewish Messiah. Many Jewish believers had a hard time accepting that God's care extended to Gentiles, too.

Paul had begun his career as a rabbi named Saul, so fervently Jewish that he persecuted fellow Jews who followed Jesus. After meeting Christ on the road to Damascus, however, he changed both his name and his attitude toward Gentiles. Paul recognized that the gospel of Christ was intended for all persons, and became a pioneer in the movement toward an inclusive church.

Paul was keenly aware that Gentile believers had formerly been "aliens from the commonwealth of Israel, and strangers to the covenants of prom- ise, having no hope and without God in the world" (v. 12). Before Christ's advent, Gentiles to whom Paul was writing may have been "God-fearers" who could stand in the outer courts of the temple compound and listen to the rabbis, but they were clearly not family.

As a result, Paul said, "You were without hope and without God in the world."

Paul has drawn a dismal picture: strangers, aliens, without God and with- out hope. But the next four words change all of that: *"But now in Christ."* Something had changed. The door was open; the wall of division was gone. "But now in Christ Jesus you who once were far off have been brought near by the blood of Christ" (v. 13). ♦

♦ **Gentiles:** Who wants to be called a "Gentile"? In today's language we sometimes apply the term, like "Philistine," to persons who are uncouth and ill mannered. In Paul's day, anyone who wasn't Jewish (and thus probably not circumcised if they were male), was considered a Gentile. The term *ethnos* (the root of our word "ethnic") was used to speak of nations or peoples other than the Hebrews.

Paul frequently contended with Jews who thought Gentiles could only be accepted as members of the church if they agreed to be circumcised, or to keep kosher in their eating habits (the letter to the Galatians was provoked by this issue). Circumcision entailed a small physical change, but it was the defining symbol of being Jewish. While circumcision is not the same kind of issue today, it reminds us of the alienation that can exist between those who are in the church, and those who are without.

Can you think of similar dividing lines that some Christians use to separate themselves from others?

Have you ever loved someone dearly, but for a while some problem came between you and led to a break in the relationship? You felt awkwardness, sadness, an uncomfortable queasiness in your stomach whenever you saw each other. You felt so far away. If you are lucky, one of you got up the nerve to apologize, or to say "I miss you, let's talk this out." And you did. You kissed and made up, or shook hands and laughed together like old times. Two persons who were far away came near to each other again.

There was a time in our lives when all of us were far away from God. We mentally looked the other way. When Sunday came, we pretended it didn't matter. When we felt an inner, spiritual emptiness, we tried to fill it up with food or alcohol or some exciting experience. But for those of us who now belong to God's family, something has changed. We have been "brought near by the blood of Christ." The door is open, the wall is gone, and our uneasy separation has given way to the warmth of Christ's embrace.

FAMILY TIES
(vv. 14-18)

Paul wants us to understand an important corollary to this truth: Our drawing near to Christ impacts our other relationships. Living close to Christ draws us near to each other within the family of God.

When I played football in high school, toward the end of each practice, the coach would blow his whistle and shout "Huddle up!" We'd all gather around the coach, who would tell us to "take a knee," and then he would review the day's practice. He would be critical when necessary and affirming whenever he could. At all times, his central interest was in team building: encouraging us to care about each other as teammates and to work together for something bigger than ourselves.

Paul has a similar concern in this text. He knows that Jesus has torn down the old fences and walls, coloring outside the cultural and religious lines of his world. Both Paul and Jesus would have us do the same. Though we may come in different shades and color in different ways, we all belong in the same picture.

Paul declared that Christ "is our peace." Jesus didn't just show us how to have peace through keeping rules or avoiding conflict. Jesus *is* our peace: we know peace because we know Christ and live in relationship with him.

This is true for both Jews and Gentiles. Through the voluntary sacrifice of his own life in the flesh, Jesus "has made both groups into one and has broken down the dividing wall, that is, the hostility between us" (v. 14). ♱ Paul was speaking primarily of barriers such as "the law with its

U **Walls:** When Paul spoke of the "dividing wall" that Christ had demolished, he may have had in mind various barriers that separated people even within Judaism. God-fearing Gentiles were allowed to pray in the outer courts of the temple in Jerusalem, but signs engraved on stone warned them not to enter the inner courts. The example at right, now in the Istanbul Museum, is written in Greek and translated "No foreigner shall enter within the forecourt and the balustrade around the sanctuary. Whoever is caught will have himself to blame for his subsequent death."

The inner section began with the Court of Women, beyond which was the Court of Israel, where only Jewish men were allowed. The actual sanctuary was reserved for the priests alone, and within the sanctuary was the Holy of Holies, which only the high priest could enter, and then just once per year.

commandments and ordinances" (v. 15a), which included rules designed to make the Jews distinct from other people. U In Christ, God was creating "one new humanity in place of the two," working to "reconcile both groups to God in one body through the cross, thus putting to death that hostility through it" (vv. 15b-16). Through Christ, we are all related.

The word translated as "put to death" comes across more strongly in Greek, where it has an active component and can be used to describe intentional murder. Even as Jesus was crucified on the cross, he purposefully wiped out engrained human hostilities and prejudices so that he could make room for love and forgiveness and harmony in humanity.

That doesn't mean we don't still face division, prejudice, and even hostility. In our churches we rarely struggle over differences between Jews and Gentiles, but

U **Commandments and ordinances?**
The phrase "commandments and ordinances" could better be translated as "commandments in decrees" (NET) or something similar: the word between "commandments" and "ordinances" is a preposition meaning "in," not the conjunction "and." This suggests that Paul had in mind the many rules the rabbis had developed to "build a fence about the law" by devising strict regulations for things such as dietary matters or the observance of the Sabbath—rules that were human in origin. Jesus nullified those.

we are aware of dividing lines based on race, age, income, marital status, education, cultural background, or other factors.

It is helpful to remember that God did not draw any of those lines, but through Jesus, God has erased them all. For those who believe, we might say, everybody is somebody's one body. That somebody is Jesus Christ. Together, we make up the one body of Christ, and we are called to love one another.

> **For Reflection:** *Can you see lines of division in your church? Are there lines between races, gender, social status, kinship, the length of one's history in the church, or other divisions? Can you identify "outsiders and insiders" in the congregation you call home? Is anything being done to address these divisions and promote true unity? If not, what could you do?*

We know it is easier to love people in the abstract than in the flesh. Most of us can resonate with the wag who said "I love humanity: it's people I can't stand!" But it is people who make up the church—people of all races, ethnicities, economic backgrounds, and political persuasions. In Christ, we are no longer strangers, no longer aliens, no longer separated from God and therefore no longer estranged from each other.

In vv. 17-18, Paul returns to the subject of peace, which he introduced in v. 14. Christ proclaimed peace to all, he said. We have equal access to God and equal responsibility to live in peace, because we all come to God through the same Spirit. ♦

> ♦ **Lines:** If you're a teacher, consider this exercise: Imagine that class members who have been members of your church for the longest time are "Jews," while more recent members are "Gentiles."
>
> Ask the "Gentiles" to reflect on what the first few Sundays felt like. Some may have felt at home from the beginning, while others may have felt "afar off."
>
> There are some churches in which former outsiders never really feel like "insiders." But, if we faithfully see ourselves as "in Christ," and welcome others who are also "in Christ," the walls that separate us can come down quickly.
>
> Perhaps some class members will share testimonies of how they came to feel "at home" in the church, and how the presence of Christ in the lives of church members facilitated their sense of acceptance.

A FIRM FOUNDATION
(vv. 19-22)

Drawing on multiple metaphors, Paul closes the chapter by emphasizing the unity of believers. We are "no longer strangers or aliens," he wrote, but "citizens with the saints and also members of the household of God" (v. 19).

In other words, we are not only fellow citizens of God's kingdom, but also brothers and sisters in God's family.

And what holds this new unity of former antagonists together? We're like a building, Paul said, that stands "upon the foundation of the apostles and prophets" (v. 20a). By "apostles," Paul refers to the eyewitnesses of the gospel who had first proclaimed it. Without their witness, there would have been no church.

By "prophets," he may have in mind the Old Testament prophets who spoke of a coming Messiah, but he was probably thinking primarily of the New Testament preachers who proclaimed the gospel of a resurrected and present Christ. Without their witness, the church could quickly fade.

Apostles and prophets may be at the foundation of the church, but "Christ Jesus himself" is the cornerstone, in whom "the whole structure is joined together and grows into a holy temple in the Lord" (v. 21).

It is Christ who holds the building together, a structure that is still growing to become the "holy temple in the Lord" that God intended. The locus of our worship is not in a physical building, no matter how magnificent, but in the fellowship of a unified people bound together by their common relationship with God in Christ.

The purpose of this spiritual building is to be "a dwelling place for God" (v. 22). Paul had used a similar metaphor in 1 Cor. 3:16, when he wrote "Do you not know that you are God's temple and that God's Spirit dwells in you?" The presence of the Holy Spirit is the mark of the true church, the animating force that binds all believers into a unified worshiping community.

Today there are many people who think of faith as a completely private thing, a personal exercise of fuzzy definition that is entirely self-centered. Paul would have had little patience for the notion of a solo faith. True spirituality, he believed, was found in the community of believers. That is where we "huddle up" to worship and grow together.

For Reflection: *How do you respond when someone tells you they are "spiritual but not religious"? Have you ever said that about yourself? Why do some people think of "being religious" as a negative thing? How can "religious" people share a more positive witness for Christ?*

THE HARDEST QUESTION

What about circumcision?

The text under consideration begins with a "then and now" construction designed to emphasize the Gentiles' position before and after Christ's work of breaking down the dividing wall so that all people might have equal access to God.

The contrast is a sharp one, made even more edgy by the author's reference to the Gentiles as being "called 'the uncircumcision' by those who are called 'the circumcision'" (v. 11).

Circumcision was one of many attributes that distinguished Jews from other peoples. They were not the first or only ones to practice the minor surgery of removing the foreskin from the penis of males. Both art and text attest that circumcision was common at various periods in Egypt, as well as among other Semitic peoples.

In the Hebrew tradition, the practice of circumcision goes back to God's call to and covenant with Abraham. Abraham was to circumcise all males in his family, including his servants, as a mark of the covenant. According to Gen. 17:14, "Any uncircumcised male who is not circumcised in the flesh of his foreskin shall be cut off from his people; he has broken my covenant." Circumcision was serious business.

During the postexilic period and into the first century, the rabbis continued to emphasize circumcision as a distinguishing mark of Judaism, with "uncircumcision" being a derogatory term for Gentiles. Greeks and Romans, on the other hand, considered circumcision to be shameful.

Within the early church, some Jewish Christians believed that Gentile believers must first become Jewish before they could be fully Christian, arguing that Gentile males should be circumcised as well as baptized. Paul saw no basis for this argument, insisting that circumcision was a Jewish practice that had nothing to do with the new covenant made possible through Christ. Paul's letter to the Galatians was largely dedicated to his arguments against "Judaizers," and is among the most heated of his writings.

Ephesians 2:11 also shows a lack of patience with those who think they are more righteous or closer to God because they are circumcised. Thus he speaks of those who proudly call themselves "the circumcision" and dismiss others as "the uncircumcision"—while noting that circumcision is "made in the flesh by human hands."

The new relationship that Gentile believers had was not the result of human doing, but of God. "But now in Christ Jesus you who once were far off have been brought near by the blood of Christ" (v. 13).

Paul used much of the same language in writing to the Colossians, where he contrasted the "spiritual circumcision" of Christ that rendered a circumcision of the flesh religiously insignificant (Col. 2:11, see also Rom. 2:28-29 and Phil. 3:2-3).

Ephesians 3:14-21

FILL UP!

I pray that, according to the riches of his glory,
he may grant that you may be strengthened in your inner being
with power through his Spirit,
and that Christ may dwell in your hearts through faith,
as you are being rooted and grounded in love.
—Ephesians 3:16-17

Is there anyone who doesn't like sunsets? As a much younger minister, while doing resort ministry at a nearby lake, I once paddled a small inflatable raft away from shore so I could lie back and watch the sun set over the open water. For more than an hour I watched as the small yellow globe sank steadily lower while appearing ever larger. Amplified and colored by increasing layers of atmosphere, the sun went through every rainbow shade between yellow and red, from gold to orange to flaming pink. When the gigantic orb finally appeared to sink beneath the waves, it was almost blood red, and I was so lost in wonder at the sight that it took me a while to realize I was in the middle of a large lake in a leaky raft, and it was dark.

Wonder can do that to you. As I get older, I'm more likely to catch the sunrise, and never fail to be enraptured as the first pink glow of dawn turns into a celestial melon playing peek-a-boo with the clouds, and ultimately into a white-hot fireball the eyes can no longer bear.

Being overcome with wonder brings the opportunity to feel most human, most vulnerable, most in tune with the power and the love of God. We can find such wonder in the miracle of birth, in the infectious giggles of children, or in the undeserved love of a spouse or a friend. We live in a world filled with so many wonders that we could all sing, with Louis Armstrong, "What a wonderful world."

Ephesians 3 includes a prayer (vv. 14-19) consisting of one long, compound sentence, followed by a doxology (vv. 20-21). As Paul prays for his friends, he is lost in wonder; not at the marvels of nature, but at the amazing grace and the powerful presence and the all-encompassing love of God. The object of his prayer is that we might all be filled up with open-faced wonder.

GOD'S AMAZING GRACE
(vv. 14-15)

In writing to the Ephesians, Paul had much to say about grace, including the familiar assertion of Eph. 2:8-9: "For by grace you have been saved through faith, and this is not your own doing; it is the gift of God—not the result of works, so that no one may boast." He went on to stress the inclusive nature of God's grace to Jews and Gentiles alike (2:11-21).

He continues that thought in chapter 3, marveling at the wonder of God's breath-taking benison: "For this reason I bow my knees before the Father, from whom every family in heaven and on earth takes its name" (vv. 14-15). ♉

The Greek text includes an intentional wordplay that is obscured in English: the word for "father" is *patera*—the root of English words such as "pa," "patriarch," and "patrimony." The word for "family" is *patria*—those who are related to the father. Paul bows before the *patera* from whom all *patria* are derived.

Theologians sometimes speak of grace that is in the background, and grace that is in the foreground. "Background grace" is all around us. Food and shelter, daylilies and dogwoods, the freshness of the air after rain are constant graces, even though we may not pause to think of them that way.

> ♉ **"For this reason . . .":** Verse 14 refers all the way back to 3:1, where Paul indicated that he was in prison for the same reason: his constant desire to win more people to Christ and to help them understand God's love for all people. He then went on to a lengthy digression about his activities and his readers' indebtedness to him before returning to his primary subject in v. 14, repeating "For this reason . . ."

There is also grace that is more in the foreground, for example, the love of a spouse who knows us inside and out and sticks with us anyway. The exuberant hug of a child is foreground grace, as is the concern of a friend when we have a need.

But beyond background grace and foreground grace is the love of a God who knows us and yet forgives us, who wants us to be part of an eternal family. It is amazing grace.

> **For Reflection:** *What are some other examples of background grace and foreground grace that are part of your daily life?*

GOD'S POWERFUL PRESENCE
(vv. 16-17)

The grace of which Paul speaks is manifest through the presence of God's Spirit in our lives. Thus Paul prayed that God might grant his readers inner strength through the power of the Spirit (v. 16).

We live in a world that craves power. Wars waged in religion's name are often really about sectarian groups seeking power over others. Special interest groups are constantly seeking political control. We long for greater income because money empowers us to do as we like without depending on others.

The power Paul is talking about is different. It is not the power to control others or even to influence people. It is the power of assurance, confidence, and mature personhood. The source of this power, Paul believed, was the indwelling presence of Christ conveyed through the Holy Spirit. Asking that the Spirit dwell in our inner being is the same thing as asking that Christ dwell in our hearts, as Paul goes on to say in v. 17, while noting that the presence of God roots and grounds us in love. 🔷

🔷 **What the readers need:** Andrew T. Lincoln finds in this text a possible motivation for Paul's letter to the Ephesians: "There may well be tendencies to rootlessness and instability, to inferiority, or at least confusion, in the face of the claims of others to knowledge and fullness, to an insufficient sense of their identity as part of the Church, and to an inadequate appreciation of the power and love available to enable them to live as God's new people, the Church."[1]

Lincoln goes on to review Paul's various intercessory requests, and in a later section concludes that: "In many ways the substance of the different requests amounts to the same thing. To be strengthened through the Spirit, to be indwelt by Christ, to be rooted in love, to know the love of Christ, and to be filled to the fullness of God involve different aspects of the experience of the same reality. Perhaps the central part of the prayer, in which the quality of love dominates, indicates that here the writer sees that reality is best summed up in the costly, self-giving love of Christ."[2]

Sadly, we've become all too familiar with prosperity preachers who completely distort the promise of God's power in our lives. "Name it and claim it," they say. "Believe and achieve! Confess and possess!" Some go so far as to claim that Christians have the authority to command God to do for us what we seek. ⚓ Such teaching is not good news, but bad theology.

⚓ **Commanding God?** In the 1990s, as the prosperity gospel was taking off, Kenneth Copeland argued that Christians have a right to make commands in the name of Jesus. "Each time you stand on the Word, you are commanding God," he said, so we should say "Lord, I want this, I name this, and I claim this in your name; Lord I want that, I name that, and I claim that in your name." He went on to say "You don't have a god in you. You are one." Likewise, Kenneth Hagin was known for saying things such as "Dogs have puppies; cats have kittens; God has little gods—claim your godhood!"[3]

But we are not little gods, and cannot achieve such status. There is only one God, and that job is taken.

What Paul wants us to have through the Holy Spirit is not the kind of power that allows us to make demands of God. Rather, it is the kind of power that grows from a relationship in which we realize that we are not God, but we also recognize the incredible truth that God loves us enough to dwell among us and bless us and guide us through the darkness of this world.

The key to experiencing the power of God's Spirit at work in us is to recognize that it is God who grants to us the power of eternal life and internal wholeness. If we have influence on other people, let it be because they admire and respect the inner peace we have and the outer love we show as children of God.

GOD'S INCLUSIVE LOVE
(vv. 18-19)

Paul has prayed that we might experience the wonder of God's amazing grace and powerful presence. Now he goes on to ask that we might "have the power to comprehend, with all the saints, what is the breadth and length and height and depth, and to know the love of Christ that surpasses knowledge," so we "may be filled with all the fullness of God" (vv. 18-19).

This sounds like a logical impossibility. Paul wants us to know something that he admits is beyond our knowing. Though he knew that none of us can fully comprehend the extent of God's love, he also knew we have the capacity to grow in our understanding.

Take note that Paul does not pray for God to love us, because God already cares for us more than we can know and has demonstrated such in Christ. We don't have to pray for God to remove any barriers between God and humankind. That's already done.

What remains to be finished is our understanding of what it means to allow God to work through us as we join with God in showing grace to others, even as we fall with Paul in prostrate worship before the God whose love draws us into an ever-new relationship.

That is our calling, but as long as we hold on to our old grudges, our ingrained prejudices, our labels and lines and divisions, estrangement remains. As we are able to understand better how deep and wide God's love is—as we draw closer to Christ and learn what it means to accept and to give unconditional and inclusive love, our worship of God will likewise grow deeper and more meaningful.

> **For Reflection**: *Allowing another driver to pull in front of us, or volunteering to do the laundry at home can be grace. Showing forgiveness or withholding judgment toward someone who said something offensive can be grace. Can you name an instance in the last week when you showed grace to someone?*

GOD'S INCREDIBLE ABUNDANCE
(vv. 20-21)

Paul closes his prayer with a joyful doxology that continues stretching the limits of our comprehension: "Now to him who by the power at work within us is able to accomplish abundantly far more than all we can ask or imagine, to him be glory in the church and in Christ Jesus to all generations, forever and ever. Amen" (vv. 20-21). 🕎

> 🕎 **Doxology:** Paul, as is typical, includes in his doxology a wish that there be glory to God. Consider these Greek words: *doxa* ("glory") and *logos* ("word"). This is how our word "doxology" is derived: it includes "words of glory" or "glory words."

Paul's prayer to this point has already gone beyond what seems possible. We may suppose Paul is whistling in the wind if he thinks God can really dwell in us and empower us and teach us to understand divine love. But Paul believed there is no end to what God can do.

The closing clause of this sentence stretches the Greek language to the breaking point. Paul stacks up double-compound superlative adverbs, as if to demonstrate that language has no capacity to explain God's love. He asks God, as the King James translation put it, to do "exceedingly abundantly above all that we ask or think." ⬇

⬇**Above and beyond:** We sometimes speak of someone going "above and beyond" what is expected. The word translated as "abundantly far more" is composed of three prepositions that mean, respectively, something like "above," "from," and "about." The combination gives the impression of something far beyond the norm. Paul is saying that God's amazing grace can accomplish far more than we could ever imagine.

God can do more than we can even dream. If you find it hard to imagine that, then you get the point. We cannot imagine the depth of God's love, the wideness of God's mercy, the fullness of God's generosity, or the reach of God's power.

If we could just begin to grasp the greatness of God—if we could incorporate into our lives just a smidgeon of God's grace, a touch of God's love, a small fraction of God's power—then we would not only be "filled up," but we would be transformed. Together, we would all be lost in wonder at the marvels of God's mercy and love, because we would see it written in our own faces and arms and hearts.

⬇**To all generations:** The doxology of v. 21 is unusual in that it's the only New Testament doxology to include the word *genea*, translated "generations," and the only one to include both singular and plural forms of the word translated "forever and ever." That word is *aiônos*, which comes into English as the word "eon."

If that should happen, we would become like magnets to others who also seek the person and the power of God. That would truly be cause for praise, and we could conclude as Paul did in v. 21: "Amen!" ⬇

For Reflection: *How can we visualize the image of something "exceedingly abundantly above all things"? Imagine a glass half filled with water, and assume that it represents our capacity for understanding. None of us are using our full capacity. Mentally pour more water into the glass until it is full, then even more until it overflows. God is able to do exceedingly abundantly above all that we can think or ask.*

THE HARDEST QUESTION

How can we comprehend "what is the breadth and length and height and depth, and to know the love of Christ that surpasses knowledge"?

Scholars have churned out many pages in an effort to untangle this prayer that stretches language to the breaking point. As Thomas B. Slater notes, some have suggested that Paul's phrasing may reflect a Stoic or astrological notion that some people could spread themselves through the cosmos, while others see it as some sort of magical formula, or an echo of Old Testament passages referring to the height and depth of creation (Ps. 139:8-10, Job 11:7-9) or a metaphor of perfection (Ezek. 48:16-17, Rev. 21:16). Yet others have argued that Paul is appealing for Christians to make every intellectual effort to understand the extent of Christ's grace.

Slater argues that such ideas miss the point that Christ is not known through intellectual achievement, but through experience: "The point of Ephesians 3:18 is not simply to intellectually know the love of Christ in its fullness but also to experience God's saving grace in its fullness. Knowledge in this instance is based on a spiritual encounter, an experience. This is most probably an experience of the Holy Spirit. Experience and reason are not mutually exclusive human phenomena but mutually inclusive."[4]

Comprehending the height, depth, breadth, and length of God comes through knowing "the love of Christ that surpasses knowledge." Here, "to know" echoes the Old Testament idiom in which "to know" someone is to know him or her by experience—an expression so intimate that it could be used of sexual intercourse ("Now the man knew his wife Eve, and she conceived …," Gen. 4:1).

In practical terms, knowing God is not an intellectual or theological enterprise. It is when we know Christ through personal experience mediated by the Spirit that we are "filled with all the fullness of God"—with as much of the height, depth, breadth, and length of divinity that our humanity can contain.

NOTES

[1] Andrew T. Lincoln, *Ephesians*, Word Biblical Commentary (Waco: Word Books, 1990), 201.

[2] Ibid., 219-20.

[3] Quoted by Leonard Sweet, "Are You Able?" *Homiletics* (July-Sept. 1994): 15-18.

[4] Thomas B. Slater, *Ephesians*, Smyth & Helwys Commentaries (Macon, GA: Smyth & Helwys, 2012), 94.

Ephesians 4:1-16

GROW UP!

There is one body and one Spirit,
just as you were called to the one hope of your calling,
one Lord, one faith, one baptism, one God and Father of all,
who is above all and through all and in all.
—Ephesians 4:4-6

Have you ever heard someone in their 30s or 40s say something like "I still don't know what I want to be when I grow up"? Was it you? Very few people feel "fully grown"—most of us would like to see more progress in our mental, psychological, or spiritual development.

You may notice a change in Paul's approach as we pass the halfway point in the letter to the Ephesians. Paul saw too many signs of immaturity in the church at Ephesus, and he urged the believers there to grow up. This shift in tenor could remind us of the old saying that the pastor "has quit preaching and gone to meddling." We usually say that sort of thing if he or she comes down hard on one of our favorite sins, or challenges our apathy, or encourages us to take stewardship seriously.

Meddling is exactly what Paul is doing in Ephesians 4. The first three chapters of Paul's touching letter find him praying for his friends. He encourages them while teaching a refresher course in basic theology. He waxes poetic and gets lost in rhapsody as he tries to express the goodness and the greatness of God.

Reading the first three chapters may leave us shouting "Amen," but Paul wants to move us from inspiration to transformation. He wants us to live up to all the lofty ideals he has exalted.

A WORTHY LIFE
(vv. 1-3)

As a "prisoner of the Lord," ✹ it was obvious that Paul took faith seriously, and he wanted his readers in Ephesus to do the same. The apostle does not only encourage or suggest or hope, but also begs his friends in Ephesus "to lead a life worthy of the calling to which you have been called" (v. 1). What could concern Paul so much that he would beg his friends to respond? What would make us more "worthy" of Christ's call to us? Several things are on his mind, and foremost among them is the importance of unity.

If diverse people are to live, work, and worship together in unity, their living must be governed by certain characteristics that promote harmony. Thus, Paul entreats the Ephesian Christians to work together "with all humility and gentleness, with patience, bearing with one another in love, making every effort to maintain the unity of the Spirit in the bond of peace" (vv. 2-3).

Humility? Patience? Not taking offense?

We might not like any of those words, any more than Paul's readers did. To some, they may sound wimpy or weak. In the Greek world, the word for humility was often used with reference to slaves. The word for "gentleness" could be used to describe a well-trained horse, as well as someone who is characteristically soft-spoken. In the New Testament, however, such words take on great virtue.

When they describe attitudes that are the result of choice, none of these terms are weak, wimpy, or pushover words. They describe people who know they are strong, but know when to bridle their strength; people who know they are right, but know when it is best to let someone else have their way; people who know they are being tested, and yet give space for others to make

---

✹ **A prisoner of the Lord:** Paul unashamedly preached the gospel, even in places where it was not popular. Local Jewish leaders were particularly threatened by his evangelizing, and they often sought ways to get Paul in trouble with governmental officials, as in Thessalonica (Acts 17:1-9).

Paul was imprisoned briefly on several occasions (2 Cor. 11:23), and after being arrested in Jerusalem (Acts 21:27-36), he was held for trial in the coastal city of Caesarea (about 58-60 CE, Acts 23–26) before appealing to the emperor and being taken to Rome, where he remained in prison for at least two years and may have been executed there (60-62 CE, Acts 27–28).

Paul described himself to the Ephesians as a "prisoner of the Lord," suggesting that he wrote this letter during one of his several imprisonments.

mistakes and remain in the sphere of their love. All of these serve the cause of promoting a fellowship known for spiritual unity and peace. ♦

What happens to church unity when everyone has to walk on eggshells because of a volatile member's temper, or when people are afraid to express their opinions for fear of being harshly judged? Unity falls to resentment. Spirits grow small instead of large.

> ♦ **The bond of love:** The themes present in Eph. 4:2-3 recall familiar Christian songs and hymns such as "We Are One in the Bond of Love" and "We Are One in the Spirit." Unity among Christians is a moving and delightful thing, well worth celebrating in song.

It may sound like a tall order to expect members in the community of faith to act with the quiet strength of humility, the controlled strength of gentleness, the wise strength of patience, and the compassionate strength of forbearance—but the church cannot experience unity without it.

> **For Reflection**: *Would a newcomer find these characteristics of humility and forbearance to be true of your church, your Sunday school class, or you as a person? Might someone who knows you better have a different opinion?*

A COMMON LIFE
(vv. 4-6)

Paul builds on the call to unity with a rousing declaration that may or may not have been original: "There is one body and one Spirit, just as you were called to the one hope of your calling, one Lord, one faith, one baptism, one God and Father of all, who is above all and through all and in all" (vv. 4-6). ♦

Many commentators have noted how much this beautiful text sounds like an ancient hymn or litany. Perhaps it was sung or recited in celebration of baptism, or as a frequent statement of faith reflecting the church's unity through the common origin of believers.

There is one God: Twice a day, faithful Jews recited a text from Deuteronomy called the

> ♦ **Seven ones:** Count how often the word "one" appears in the hymnic text of vv. 4-6. In most translations, you'll find seven—a number that often denotes completeness or perfection in biblical use. Do you think the sevenfold repetition is intentional?

shema, and it begins with the words "Hear, O Israel: The LORD is our God, the LORD alone." There is one Spirit, Paul says, one Lord, one God and Father of all. The unity of the church begins with the unity of its creator.

And, Paul says, we come to know that one God through the same expression of trust: "there is one faith." Some people come to faith in Christ through an emotional experience that wrenches the heart and sets the soul free in a torrent of joy and tears, while other persons absorb faith through a quiet childhood of consistent Bible teaching and family prayers and church worship.

We come to Christ in different ways, at different ages, and we may express our love for Christ in different manners, but we all share the same faith. We have confessed our sins and trusted in the amazing grace of God, so that we can all say "by grace we are saved through faith." We have one faith.

We worship one God, then, and we have come to know God through one faith. We also share in at least one other sign of unity: the expression of our faith through the experience of baptism.

We do not know if everyone in Paul's day was baptized by the same mode, but every baptism served the same purpose as an outward, public profession of faith in Jesus Christ, a sacred ritual of renewal and rebirth.

Baptism is special. That is why Baptists can be downright fanatical about it. While most of us recognize that sprinkling or pouring can be legitimate modes for baptism, we also believe that baptism by immersion so beautifully conveys the symbolism Jesus intended that we want everyone else to experience it as we have—and as a believer rather than as a baby.

Remember these ties that bind, Paul says: We all worship one God, revealed to us through the same Spirit. We all came to know Christ through one faith. We are joined together in one baptism. God has created the church as a unity. Those Christians who live worthy of their calling will not foster division, but will nurture unity.

A GIFTED LIFE
(vv. 7-16)

As we live and work and express our unity within the church, Paul wants us to remember that we are nevertheless unique individuals who have been blessed in particular ways so that we may all serve the one church in different ways according to our ability.

Christ has given grace-gifts to each of us, Paul says (v. 7). The Greek word for "grace" is *charis*. The word for "spiritual gifts" is *charismata*. So, a "spiritual gift" is really a "grace gift." The grace that brings us into fellowship with Christ is a gift, but that is not Christ's only gift to us. He has blessed us all with unique spiritual gifts that enable us to serve him better.

When we come to vv. 8-10, they seem to interrupt the text and sidetrack us from Paul's discussion of spiritual gifts. (For an explanation of these verses, see "The Hardest Question" on page 42.)

In vv. 11-13, Paul describes some of the spiritual gifts he has in mind. We note that this is one of several lists of spiritual gifts in Paul's writings (compare Rom. 12:6-8; 1 Cor. 12:4-11, 27-28), and none of them are exhaustive. The gifts Paul mentions here are mostly associated with leadership abilities, while others emphasize character traits such as love, faith, generosity, or hospitality. ⬥

Where leadership is concerned, believers may be gifted or categorized as apostles, prophets, evangelists, pastors, or teachers, but all should work toward the same end: They are to "to equip the saints for the work of ministry, for building up the body of Christ" (v. 12). That comes through growth in

⬥ **Gifted leaders:** The list of gifts in v. 11 includes the ability to serve as apostles, prophets, evangelists, pastors, and teachers. The term "apostle" is generally reserved for persons who followed Jesus during his earthly life and had a direct call from him. Paul considered himself an apostle because he had seen Christ and received his call in a vision.

In the New Testament as in the Hebrew Bible, a prophet was not a fore-teller so much as a forth-teller: someone who could interpret the human situation and relate it to the divine will, challenging God's people to live both responsibly and with hope. Good preachers or writers who challenge the church on important issues could be considered prophets.

An evangelist is one who proclaims the good news of the gospel. While Paul may have had in mind itinerant evangelists who were particularly gifted at persuading others to follow Christ, any person whose life or words inspire others to respond to the gospel could be considered an evangelist.

The two words "pastors and teachers" are governed by a single article in the Greek, leading some to translate them as "pastor-teachers," or to assume that "pastors" and "teachers" refer to the same people. While good pastors should be good teachers, not all teachers are pastors, so it is best to consider them separately.

The word translated "pastor" (*poimenas*) is the standard word for "shepherd." A pastor is entrusted with a spiritual flock whom he or she is to love, guide, feed, and care for as members of the church. While pastors may and should teach, others also play important roles in explaining the scriptures and helping church members understand their place and role in the kingdom of God.

unity, in faith, and in the knowledge of Christ. The goal is to become more spiritually mature; more like Christ (v. 13).

Observe that Paul does not stress the growth of the church in numbers or in financial or political clout, but in unity that is patterned after Christ. If members of the church grow in oneness of spirit and love and service to Christ, then other aspects of growth will follow naturally.

In closing this appeal, Paul shifts to a metaphor of the church as a body in which members experience growth in maturity, or what is often called "spiritual formation." Evidence of such growth or formation is seen as we accept our role as contributing members of the body of Christ. We have diverse roles to play in keeping with our gifts, but we all fall under the leadership of one head, and the head is Christ (vv. 14-16).

The result, Paul says, is the building up of the body "in love" (v. 16). When we work in unity, we learn to love. When we truly love, we will strive for unity.

> **For Reflection**: *When you look over Paul's recounting of spiritual gifts that relate to leadership, do you find any that feel like a fit for you? Can you name ways in which you exercise some of these gifts in your daily or congregational life?*

THE HARDEST QUESTION

To where did Christ descend?

The statement in vv. 8-10 has often been misunderstood. Most modern translations add parentheses on either side of vv. 9-10, indicating that they are an explanation of the quotation in v. 8: "Therefore it is said, 'When he ascended on high he made captivity itself a captive; he gave gifts to his people.'"

Paul explains this saying in vv. 9-10: When it says, "He ascended," what does it mean but that he had also descended into the lower parts of the earth? He who descended is the same one who ascended far above all the heavens, so that he might fill all things.

Let's begin by taking a closer look at v. 8, which appears to be a loose quotation of Ps. 68:18: "You ascended the high mount, leading captives in your train and receiving gifts from people, even from those who rebel against the LORD God's abiding there."

A Jewish tradition associated this text with Moses, who led the Israelites out of captivity and ascended to the top of Mt. Sinai (some argued that he ascended to heaven) to receive the commandments of God.

Notice how loosely Paul treats the text. First, he gives it a clearly Christological interpretation: After his resurrection, Jesus ascended "on high," not leading former captives as Moses did, but taking captive the power of evil that had enslaved believers. Then, instead of receiving gifts from people, as in Ps. 68:18, Christ gave gifts to his people, namely the gifts of the Spirit that Paul goes on to discuss in vv. 11-13.

But what about the parenthetical expression in vv. 9-10? Many readers have assumed that this relates to an early belief that Jesus descended into Sheol between his death and resurrection (as 1 Pet. 3:18-20 may imply). Some presume that Jesus preached to Jews who died before his time and led them from their limbo-like state of captivity to a new home in heaven.

This is probably not the correct interpretation.

Paul's emphasis is on Christ's ascent to heaven, from which position he gave gifts to his people. He notes that Christ could not ascend to heaven if he had not first descended to earth, so this is most likely a reference to Jesus' incarnation. The expression "lower parts of the earth" (NRSV) could also be translated "to the lower regions, namely, the earth" (NET) or "to the lowest level, down to the very earth" (NEB). Thus, Christ's descent was not to Sheol, but to earth. In his life on earth, from birth to death, Jesus had descended to the same level of reality in which we live. From there, having conquered death, he ascended in power to rain gifts of the Spirit upon his people.

Ephesians 4:25-5:2

BUILD UP!

Therefore be imitators of God, as beloved children,
and live in love, as Christ loved us and gave himself up for us,
a fragrant offering and sacrifice to God.
—Ephesians 5:1-2

D
o you like to have your toes mashed? Today's text may sound more like diatribe than dialogue, as Paul minces no words in calling for the struggling church members in Ephesus to put their lying, stealing, cheating days behind them and to take on the character of Christ.

No doubt, this text has given rise to many toe-stomping sermons designed to put sinful Christians in their place. Forty years ago, I preached such sermons. Modeling the style of a former pastor, I stepped on every questionable toe I could find.

Surprisingly, many parishioners affirm such no-holds-barred preaching. Some people have a spiritually masochistic streak and seem to like being told how bad they are. Others enjoy hearing how bad everyone else is. ⬇

⬇ **That's tellin' 'em:** An old preacher's story speaks of a mountain church whose fellowship included a rather incorrigible character who always assumed the sermons were intended for everyone else, but not for him. On the way out, he would often say: "Preacher, you sure told 'em today!"

The pastor was frustrated by this, but a Sunday came when the snow was so deep that this particular man was the only one to show up for church. The pastor preached his sermon anyway, confident that his crusty parishioner would take the message to heart, but as he left that morning, the man shook his hand and said: "Preacher, if they'd 'a been here, you sure woulda told 'em!"

Some church folk like that kind of preaching because they've been told all their lives that they are bad, and hardball sermons reinforce their understanding of reality.

Others find rub-it-in-your-face preaching to be cathartic. They know they have sinned during the week, and getting verbally whipped for it on Sunday is sort of like taking their punishment. They feel better when it's over.

Others feel attacked, and don't come back.

While Paul's admonitions in Eph. 4:25–5:2 are plain-spoken, they are not unkind. He is able to "call a spade a spade" without bashing people with a shovel. He simply points out that believers should move past harmful habits and unhealthy lifestyles to take on the goodness and love of Christ.

We do this not in order to become Christians but because we are already followers of Christ, called to live up to our names.

SPEAKING THE TRUTH
(4:25)

A baptism theme runs throughout Ephesians 4. When we are baptized, we symbolically strip off the old life of sin and bury it in the waters of baptism. We are then raised to a new life in Christ Jesus. Paul believed that Christ has the power to transform our hearts and lives, to give us a new nature, to make of us the best people imaginable. When Paul talks to Christians, he does not tell them to go and find some goodness somewhere and put it on, but rather to live up to the goodness that is already in them as children of God. ♉

You may remember the line from Robert Burns' poem, "To a Louse":

O wad some pow'r the giftie gie us,
to see oursels as ithers see us.

Perhaps we could rephrase that a bit and see Paul's goal as this:

O would some power come help persuade us,
to be ourselves as God has made us!

Paul's concern is that all believers learn to reach their potential as the children of God. He uses such straightforward language because some believers don't fully know who they are, and so he finds it helpful to explain to them what the Christian nature is all about.

When Paul begins this text with "So, then ..." (NRSV), he is building on all that comes before, and in particular 4:17-24, where he had pointed out that redeemed Christians are different people than they were before meeting Christ, and their lives should reflect the change. Paul was convinced that if we truly become Christians, everything changes.

An old saying insists: "You can tell a real cowboy by the way he walks." The same is true of a Christian, though it is not a bow-legged gait that identifies us, but Christ's love in our living. Paul knew that the most obvious difference in the Christian's life is seen in language, attitudes, and personal relationships.

We must put off falsehood and speak truthfully as members of Christ's body, Paul says. That's not hard to understand. Truth telling is essential for personal integrity and for the health of the larger body.

If we lie to each other, then we can no longer trust each other, and we won't be one body anymore. We will be fractured, suspicious, divided. We can't have congregational unity if we don't have trust. We can't have trust if we are not truthful with each other. These things are obvious.

⬇ **Less than you are:** Paul's call for believers to live up to who they are in Christ calls to mind a moving scene in Disney's movie *The Lion King*. After the death of the lion king Mufasa, his son, prince Simba, runs away for fear that he will be blamed for his father's death. Far away from the pride lands, he finds a home in the jungle with a warthog (Pumba) and a meercat (Timon). They teach him to have a "no worries" attitude toward life, which is epitomized in the song "Hakuna Matata." It's a fun song, and it's nice to imagine that we have no worries, but that is also dreaming.

When the pride lands are in danger of extinction because of Simba's wicked uncle Scar's incompetent and selfish rule, Simba's childhood friend Nala comes looking for help. She is surprised to find Simba, now grown into a strong and powerful lion, enjoying a life of ease, eating bugs and worms in the jungle. She begs him to return as the rightful king, to confront the evil Scar, and to help his people. But Simba is hesitant. He's not so sure he can do it. He is still afraid of what might happen, afraid that he might be blamed for his father's death. And so, he remains paralyzed and inactive.

One cloudy day, Simba is sitting beside a still pond, struggling with the choices before him, when he sees in the clouds a vision of his father's face. In a deep and authoritative voice, Mufasa speaks a challenge to his son: "You have become less than you are."

Think about that for a minute: "You have become less than you are." Could that be said of you? Can it be said of me? Have we so given in to our culture and our habits and our selfishness that we have become less than God made us to be? Are we content to stay that way?

For Reflection: *Most of us don't know a lot of cowboys, and some of us may not immediately understand that the saying about the way cowboys walk refers to the bow-legged stance common to people who spend hours each day in the saddle.*

Try updating the saying to get the point across in more contemporary terms by filling in the blanks in this sentence: "You can tell a real _____ by the way he or she _____."

MANAGING ANGER
(4:26-28)

Now Paul moves to a subject that is a little harder to deal with. "Be angry but do not sin," he says. Paul knew that everyone gets angry. Even Jesus got angry. The issue is not whether we will experience anger, but how we manage it.

What do you do with *your* anger? Many of us try to suppress it, because somewhere along the way a well-meaning parent or teacher or friend has told us that it is wrong to be angry, that we shouldn't get angry, that we're in danger of hellfire if we ever get angry.

Paul knew better. Getting angry when we are wronged is as natural as getting wet when it rains. Of course, most of us don't stand out in the rain because we like getting soaked, or wear our feelings on our sleeves so we'll have more reasons to be angry.

Some people are so insecure that they are constantly angry, thinking everyone is out to get them. Others with the same insecurities don't get mad at all, because they think so little of themselves that they figure they deserve whatever happens.

Paul offers a better way. Whatever the cause of our anger, we can set a good example by managing our anger in ways that are helpful and not harmful.

In essence, Paul is saying "It's okay to be angry—just don't let your anger lead you to sin." There are mature and appropriate ways to express our anger. These do not include physical violence or character assassination or passive-aggressive behavior designed to make others miserable. We can learn to say what needs to be said in a way that is both kind and clear. We can channel that excess energy into something that is *con*structive rather than *de*structive.

That is why Paul says "do not let the sun go down on your anger" (4:26). The longer we fuel an inner rage, the more it eats at us. The longer we carry a grudge, the heavier it gets. When we finally express that anger, the more likely it is to be ugly.

It is appropriate that Paul mentions stealing in conjunction with anger (4:28). Thievery can be understood as an unhealthy expression of anger. Those who steal from other people or from their workplace are acting out an inner anger. Those who steal others' virtue and freedom through rape or abuse are allowing inner rage to control them. For whatever reasons—a life of poverty or abuse at home, the experience of prejudice at the hands of others, a history of being misunderstood—many people come to believe that others have not treated them rightly. Some may attempt to "make things right" or get even by taking what they want. Theft is a prime example of how *not* to manage one's anger.

> **For Reflection:** *What things are most likely to pique your anger? Have you found any positive or constructive ways to express or work out your vexation?*

ADJUSTING ATTITUDES
(4:29-32)

Paul now moves on to a series of specific instructions, all of which have to do with our basic attitudes toward life and toward others. He begins by telling us to speak in wholesome ways that benefit others (4:29).

Ugly words can hurt. They can destroy self-esteem in a child or an adult. In contrast, helpful and encouraging words can do amazing things. When Paul spoke of "building others up according to their needs," he drew a wonderful picture. Our words can build up self-esteem and self-confidence in others. Our words can be a blessing that make people smile. Our words can affirm that which is best in people and help them to believe in themselves.

Christ calls us to live obediently, empowered by the Spirit. Thus, Paul tells the Ephesians not to "grieve the Holy Spirit of God, with which you were marked with a seal for the day of redemption" (4:30). The Spirit of God lives in us, as a foretaste and promise of our ultimate redemption. The presence of harmful, hateful attitudes is an affront to the indwelling Spirit, who grieves with every spiteful word we speak.

Believers are not to be characterized by bitterness, brawling, slander or malice, Paul said (4:31). Faithful followers of Jesus do not fight either in public or behind each other's backs. Those who have the Spirit do not hold grudges, keep score, or use other people as steppingstones for personal advancement. The presence of such attitudes has led to division and a lack of effectiveness in too many churches.

⚱ **Bitterness and brawling:** Here's a closer look at the unhelpful behaviors mentioned in 4:31.

"Bitterness" is from the word *pikros*. As in English, it could describe a bitter root or bitter fruit, or be used metaphorically for a bitter spirit, bitter speech, and so forth.

The word for "wrath" is *thumos*, which can refer to fierce indignation, passion, or rage.

The term tamely translated as "anger" in v. 31 is the noun form of the verb (*orgizesthe*) used in v. 25. It comes from a root that can describe plants or fruits swelling with juice, about to burst. It is similar to the Hebrew way of indicating a furious response by saying someone's "nose swells." In this context, wrath is the kind of anger that may result in an outburst and spew all over others.

The fourth word on the list, translated as "wrangling" in the NRSV, is *krauge*. It describes a noisy or attention-getting clamor, outcry, or uproar that is designed to disturb the peace.

"Slander" comes from the root *blasphemia*, which can refer to slander against other humans as well as blasphemy against God. It describes reproachful speech about another that is harmful to that person. We normally think of slanderous speech as being false, but even partial truths can be twisted in a harmful way.

Paul wraps up the string of speech and attitudinal behaviors with a summary reference to "all malice" (*pasa kakia*), a generic expression for anger that has an evil or harmful intent.

Forgoing bitterness, we are called to be kind, compassionate, and forgiving (4:32). ⚱ Why? Because we remember how God has been kind to us, how Christ demonstrated selfless love, how we have been forgiven. Gratitude leads us to reflect those same attitudes.

IMITATING CHRIST
(5:1-2)

This is how the Christian lives. We don't get our satisfaction from bitterness or our thrills from putting others down. We find joy in kindness, and fulfillment in forgiveness. By this, we bring joy to the Spirit who lives in us, and not grief. We become "imitators of God" who live a life of love, "just as Christ loved us and gave himself up for us" (5:1-2).

This is not something we can do on our own. But, because God has loved us and blessed us and in Christ has forgiven us, we can respond with love and blessing and forgiveness toward others. Through our trust in Christ, through our baptism, through our fellowship with other believers, we have experienced life as the children of God. This enables us to show love and forgiveness and grace to others—to be imitators of God who "live in love" as Christ taught us to do.

👆 **Kindness and compassion:** If we're going to study the negative words of v. 31, let's also take a look at the more positive characteristics of v. 32, where Paul says we should be kind, tenderhearted, and forgiving.

The word for "kind" is *chrestoi*, which can mean "useful" or "virtuous," but also has connotations of being easy, manageable, or pleasant. People who are kind do helpful things for others, and in an agreeable way.

"Tenderhearted" comes from the delightful word *eusplangchnos*, which literally describes good (the prefix *eu*) bowels (*splangchnon*). In Paul's day, people commonly thought of the bowels, rather than the heart, as the seat of compassion or deep feelings. Even today, we speak of "gut feelings," and when we get upset we know how it affects our stomachs. Still, we're more likely to speak metaphorically of the heart as our most compassionate organ.

The word translated "forgive" is *charizomenoi*, from the same root that gives rise to our words "charisma" and "charismatic." The word for "grace" is *charis*. The verbal form, then, means "to show grace" or "to show favor," which we can also translate as "forgive."

For Reflection: *Those who truly imitate Christ also demonstrate the presence of Christ to others. Who in your life has demonstrated Christ most effectively to you? Can you name different people who influenced you positively at different stages of life? Is it likely that anyone else would name you as having been a Christ-like blessing to them?*

THE HARDEST QUESTION

How do we interpret the insistence in v. 30 that believers should not "grieve the Holy Spirit, with which you were marked for the day of redemption"?

First, we note that this is not equivalent to "blasphemy against the Holy Spirit"—though that would indeed be grievous—as spoken of in Matt. 12:31-32, and sometimes thought of as "the unforgiveable sin." That is a different matter.

Before Jesus ascended to heaven, he promised to send the Holy Spirit to empower his followers. The descent of the Spirit upon Jewish believers at Pentecost (Acts 2) and upon Gentile believers in the "Gentile Pentecost" (Acts 10:44-48) was seen as a confirmation of Christ's promise. The presence of the Spirit in each believer serves as a reminder—like a molten wax seal on a letter—that we have been marked by God as God's people, now living on earth but citizens of another land, to be entered at the "day of redemption."

Paul's admonition comes within the context of speech: We are not to speak evil and harmful words that tear others down, but words of kindness that build people up (v. 29). Our words do not just impact other people, however. If the Spirit lives in us, it would cause sorrow for God to hear us speak wicked words: we should be careful what we say.

I still like the way the late Malcolm Tolbert, one of my beloved seminary professors, explained this back in 1979:

> Many people watch their language in the church building because they think of it as God's house, the place where God is. This was not Paul's thinking. For Paul, each believer is a temple of God's Spirit. Wherever the Christian is, the Spirit is there. The believer always should be aware, therefore, that his or her whole life is lived in the Spirit's presence. What the believer says on the golf course or in the barber shop or in the grocery store should be just as responsible as what that person says in the church building—perhaps even more so.[1]

NOTE

[1]Malcolm Tolbert, *Ephesians: God's New People* (Nashville: Convention Press, 1979), 105.

Ephesians 5:15-21

LIVE UP!

Be subject to one another out of reverence for Christ.
—Ephesians 5:21

D o others consider you something of a fashionista? As much as we may think of ourselves as "being our own persons," our fashion choices tend to be influenced by what other people are wearing, by the colors and styles that are popular at a given time. After all, that's what the stores have for sale.

As I was growing up with two younger brothers, our family clothing budget didn't allow for a lot of cutting-edge fashion. But, whenever a new fad came along, my mother would get out the sewing machine and make at least one stylish item so we wouldn't be left out. The first clothing fad I remember was calypso pants (like capris, but for boys). I was glad that didn't last long. My pair was black, and the only time I happily wore them was as part of a pirate costume at Halloweeen.

In junior high school, all the boys were wearing plaid shirts that looked like they were made from checked tablecloths. (Some of them may have been.) My mother made me a blue one. The next year, as the Beach Boys became popular, it was "surfer shirts," which had no collar, just a little piping around the neck. Mine was yellow.

I was a junior in high school when the Beatles popularized Nehru jackets, and my mother found some light blue satin material for mine. With a white turtleneck, white pants, and a fake silver chain, I felt like the cat's meow.

I confess that as a young preacher, my closet once held two polyester leisure suits with psychedelic shirts sporting long pointed collars. After that, I decided that fashion would have to move along without me.

It's natural for us to imitate what others do: Peer pressure is a powerful thing, and not just when it comes to clothes.

That is precisely the problem Paul is addressing in Ephesians 5. He knows the tendency of all people—including church people—to follow the crowd and imitate the ways of the world. With sharply worded arguments, Paul attempts to turn the equation around. He wants his readers to live up to their calling by becoming imitators—but of Christ, rather than their neighbors. "Therefore be imitators of Christ, beloved children," he writes (5:1). Paul challenges his readers to avoid becoming *imitation* Christians, and to become *imitating* Christians. Our motto is not to "Be like Mike," as in the old Nike commercial, but to "Be like Christ!"

LIVE CAREFULLY
(vv. 15-16)

Our text begins with v. 15, but it is helpful to take note of what has come before. The chapter opens with a challenge for believers to imitate Christ by demonstrating the same kind of sacrificial love toward others that we find in Christ (vv. 1-2).

In vv. 3-7, Paul lists a catalog of sins that believers may have practiced in their former lives, but should now avoid, because "once you were darkness, but now in the Lord you are light," and should "live as children of the light" (v. 8), which reveals "what is good and right and true" (v. 9).

Thus, Christ-followers should seek to understand what pleases God and choose those behaviors and live in such a way that they will be unashamed for their deeds to be seen in the light (vv. 10-13). Quoting bits and pieces from a variety of Old Testament verses, perhaps, then adding words of his own, Paul intones "Therefore it says, 'Sleeper, awake! Rise from the dead, and Christ will shine on you'" (v. 14). 🔯

🔯 **A composite quote?** No Old Testament scripture matches what Paul claims to be quoting in 5:14, though several texts in Isaiah contain similar phrases. Isaiah 26:19 includes the line "O dwellers in the dust, awake and sing for joy!" In Isa. 51:7, the prophet calls on Jerusalem to "Rouse yourself!" Similarly, Isa. 52:1 begins with "Awake, awake, put on your strength, O Zion!" And, Isa. 60:1 says "Arise, shine, for your light has come."

Paul tended to quote scripture loosely and adapt it to his own purposes. For example, if he saw it as a prediction or foreshadowing of Christ, as here, he might insert "Christ" into the text. Modern exegetes would shudder at such a casual approach, but Paul was reflecting typical rabbinic practice of his day.

Those who wake and walk in the light understand that we are called to make careful use of every moment that God gives us. We are to be wise rather than unwise (v. 15), Paul says, good stewards of the life we've been given, aware that our time is limited. ♦

♦ **Wake up and live!** The late Bob Goode, who served many years as preschool children's specialist for the Baptist State Convention of North Carolina, experienced a serious illness during his seminary days. Later, he wrote a powerful essay in which he reflected on the lessons he had learned from his brush with death. Some of his thoughts are well worth sharing. Early in the essay, Bob had called to mind the popular children's bedtime prayer that begins "Now I lay me down to sleep." Here's what he said:

> I was in the hospital in the midst of a life-threatening illness when one evening I found myself saying inwardly the little prayer's most poignant line: "If I should die before I wake."
>
> Suddenly, I knew that what was troubling me was not so much the thought of dying, but of dying before I had fully waked from the slumber of my life. I realized that what the prayer says is: "Wake up and live, for time is flying." I promised myself passionately that never again would I take a moment of life for granted.
>
> In that flash of illumination, I thought of what a profound word "waking" is, how close to the roots of life. The dictionary says that "to awaken" means not only to "be roused from sleep," but also "to rise to action." In short, it is to be born again into life.
>
> The adult, like the child, should rise from sleep with spring in his heart; should, and so rarely does. Suppose we counted how many hours there were in a recent week when we moved about like children, antenna out for the winds of heaven, touching, hearing, looking, as though morning had just dawned on the earth for the first time. How many would there be?

Indeed, we should be "making the most of the time" (NRSV), or in the familiar King James Version, we should "redeem the time" we have in a world dominated by evil (v. 16).

The expression comes from what seems to be an unusual compound word. The Greek prefix *ex-* typically means "out of." The verb *agorazo* means "to buy," because it is something you do in the marketplace, the *agora*. Paul uses the combination *exagorazo*, which suggests taking something out of the marketplace—out of the ordinary. To "redeem the time" is to look beyond the mundane ticking of the clock and remember that we are citizens of eternity, "taking advantage of every opportunity" (NET) to live as Jesus lived. ♦

♦ **Really live:** Here's the concluding section of Bob Goode's essay. He didn't write it as a commentary on Eph. 5:16, but it suits perfectly as a reminder that we are called to live each day fully awake and alive to the possibilities before us:

. . . to be awake . . . is the task of all of us before we die. But few people live their lives so. Instead, we drift along on the surface of things, dazed and confused like dreamers, only half-alive. Then, there comes a day when the shortness of time is upon us like a dark end.

What we hoped to do with our lives has not been done; the things we wanted to say have not been said; the people to whom we wanted to express our love have never received it; the wrongs we have done have not been made up for; the talents we have, have not been used.

It almost seems as though we have done it on purpose; as though drifting is what we really want. But it is not. What we really want is to live while we live. We want to wake before we die . . . Inevitably we live between light and dark, life and death. Daily we come out of the thicket of darkness, live in the bright bowl of the sun, and return again to the fall of night. "Now I lay me down to sleep."

When we have lived a day richly and warmly, running in the sunlight, laughing and loving, then night comes sweetly and without regret. Perhaps that other night, that longer night we call death, will come sweetly, too, if we have spent our life so that it blessed us and the others around us; come sweetly and bring, like all the nights we've known, a new and fresh awaking.

To live each day to the full, to live in the light, to make the most of every present moment while remembering we are citizens of eternity—that is what it means to "redeem the time."

LIVE WISELY
(v. 17)

Paul had challenged his readers to live "not as unwise people but as wise" in v. 15, and here he returns to that theme: "So do not be foolish, but understand what the will of the Lord is" (v. 17). The NET translation opts for a different sentence construction that makes the point more clearly: "For this reason do not be foolish, but be wise by understanding what the Lord's will is."

To be wise, Paul implies, is to seek understanding of God's will. To live wisely is to live according to God's will. And what is God's will? Paul has already made that clear: that we imitate Christ by living in love, the same kind of unselfish love that Jesus modeled and taught his disciples, as John's gospel recalls: "I give you a new commandment, that you love one another. Just as I have loved you, you also should love one another. By this everyone will know that you are my disciples, if you have love for one another" (John 13:34-35).

> **For Reflection**: *Do you think of yourself as wise, according to Paul's definition? How do you determine what you believe to be the Lord's will for you?*

LIVE IN THE SPIRIT
(vv. 18-21)

Christians are directed toward God's will and empowered to love when they open their lives to the presence of Christ's Spirit. Thus, Paul challenges readers to forgo spirits in favor of the Spirit; and to avoid being drunk on wine but be filled with the Spirit of Christ (v. 18).

It's not self-evident in most English translations, but Paul's challenge to be filled with the Spirit is followed by five participles that appear to describe the results of a life that is in touch with the Spirit of Christ: "speaking," "singing," "making music" (v. 19); "giving thanks" (v. 20); and "submitting" (v. 21). 🕎

⬢ **The end, or the beginning?** Should v. 21 be seen as the end of the paragraph that begins in v. 18, or the beginning of the next? The NAS95, NET, HCSB, and even the KJV see a connection between vv. 18-20 and v. 21, regarding v. 21 as the last phrase in Paul's reflection on living in the Spirit.

The NRSV and NIV, in contrast, interpret v. 21 as beginning a new section on submission. To do so, however, they give the participle "submitting" an imperatival sense: "Be subject" (NRSV) or "Submit" (NIV). One possible reason for this is that the next verse, typically translated as "Wives, be subject to your husbands as you are to the Lord," has no verb in some of the earliest and best witnesses, so "submit" has to be supplied or the sense of it carried over from the previous verse. Other important manuscripts do include a second- or third-person imperative form of the verb in v. 22, but text-critics generally regard the shorter form to be more original.

Beginning with v. 21, Paul begins a section on "house rules," counseling husbands and wives to live in mutual submission to one another, children to obey their parents, and servants to be submissive to their masters (5:21-6:9).

One should not try to stretch Paul's participles to draw out five very different behaviors. The first three, for example, go together: speaking to one another in the words of psalms and hymns most commonly takes place in the context of music, "singing and making melody to the Lord in your hearts" (v. 19). ⬢

Notice the two-pronged nature of this very important element of worship: The words of our "psalms and hymns and spiritual songs" are directed both to each other and to the Lord. As we sing powerful words from the heart, we not only praise God, but we also encourage one another. This is why I believe the musical aspect of worship is most meaningful when the accompanists' contribution does not drown out the voices of the people. Whether the people around me are in tune or off key, I like to hear the people sing: it encourages me, even as I believe it pleases God.

⬢ **Speaking, or singing?** The NRSV begins v. 19 with "as you sing psalms...," but the verb (*la--lountes*) virtually always refers to speaking or talking, not singing. We often read from the psalms in worship without singing them, and sometimes recite hymnic litanies. First-century Christians are likely to have done the same.

A primary purpose of our singing to each other and to God is that of giving thanks to God. This is not limited to worship: Paul implies that we should do this "at all times."

And for what do we give thanks? The Greek simply says "all"—the word *pantōn* can be either neuter or masculine. Most modern translations take it as neuter and translate "for everything" or "for all things," but the NET opts for the masculine form, which can refer to all persons, and suggests that we should thank God "for each other." Since v. 19 sets the context of speaking or singing to each other as well as to God, it is not inappropriate to carry this forward and think of thanking God for each other. In either case, "all things" could include "each other."

The final participle acts as a nice segue to the next section, which deals with the mutual submission that should characterize Christian relationships, including marriage. Those who are being filled by the Spirit demonstrate this in "submitting to one another out of reverence for Christ" (v. 21, NET), which is really another way of saying "be imitators of God, as beloved children, and live in love" (v. 1). We can't follow Jesus' command to "love one another as I have loved you" unless we are willing to put others' needs before our own, trusting that our fellow believers will love us in the same way.

> **For Reflection**: *When we hear Paul's challenge and we examine our lives, what do we see? Are we imitation Christians who carry the name but not the substance, or imitating Christians who model our lives on the life of Christ, seeking daily to walk in the love and the light of Jesus, in the power of the Spirit, to the glory of God?*

THE HARDEST QUESTION

What's the difference between "psalms, hymns, and spiritual songs"?

The triple reference to "psalms, hymns, and spiritual songs" is found in both Eph. 5:19 and Col. 3:16. Some old-line churches, especially in the Reformed tradition, believe the only singing that should take place in worship should be from the book of Psalms, a practice called "Exclusive Psalmnody." Defenders of this tradition argue that "psalms, hymns, and spiritual songs" are simply three synonyms, piled together for emphasis, but all referring to the Old Testament psalms rather than post-biblical creations.

Examples of such "synonymia" can be found in scripture. Exodus 1:7, for example, says the children of Israel "were fruitful, and increased, and multiplied"—all different ways of noting that the population increased significantly. The argument that "psalms, hymns, and spiritual songs" must all refer to the biblical psalms is a forced interpretation, however.

The first meaning of the word for "psalm" (*psalmos*) is "a striking" or "twanging" of musical strings or chords, the instrumentation for a song. The word came to be used with reference to the biblical psalms. In the Septuagint, the early Greek translation, the Hebrew word *mizmor* (which we translate as "psalm") is usually rendered by *psalmos*.

The book of Psalms consists of several different types of psalms, including hymns (*hymnos* in Greek)—note that the words for both "psalm" and "hymn" are very similar in Greek and English. Although some people think of hymns as limited to songs of praise, the hymn form could also be used for other purposes: the Old Testament (and not only in the book of Psalms) contains both hymns of praise and hymns of lament. In Eph. 5:19, however, the context is clearly one of thanksgiving to God, so it is likely that Paul was thinking mainly of hymns of praise.

The New Testament includes examples of hymns that appear to have been used in the early church. Mary's song in Luke 1:46-55, often called "The Magnificat," is in hymnic form, as is the song of Zechariah in Luke 1:67-79 ("The Benedictus") and Simeon's praise after greeting the infant Jesus in Luke 2:29-32, known in liturgical circles as the "Nunc Dimittis."

When Jesus and his disciples "sang a hymn" before leaving after the Last Supper, it was almost certainly not "Blest Be the Tie That Binds," but all or part of what is called "The Hallel," or Psalms 113-118, commonly sung by observant Jews at major festivals including the Passover.

Philippians 2:6-11 is clearly poetic and often considered to be an early hymn. It is the sort of thing that Paul and Silas might have sung, along with Hebrew psalms, while in prison (Acts 16:25).

Thus, "psalms" and "hymns" could refer to the biblical psalms, but it's not necessary to think the early church limited their singing to the book of Psalms.

"Spiritual songs" incorporates the generic Greek word for "song," *'od*—from which the English word "ode" derives—and the word *pneumaticos*, the adjectival form of the word *pneuma*, or "spirit."

A spiritual song, then, could refer to any song that deals with spiritual things, though some argue that it describes only songs that are inspired by the Spirit. Interpreters who take this track fork into various directions. Some insist that only the scriptures can claim to be inspired by the Spirit, thus "spiritual song" must refer to the biblical psalms alone. Others think of "spiritual songs" as charismatic utterances, perhaps in tongues, that result from worshiping "in the spirit."

There is no compelling evidence limiting us to either of those views, and a middle way is also possible. A "spiritual song" is any song that concerns itself with spiritual matters, or that emerges from the life of one who seeks to be filled with the Spirit. This is precisely what Paul suggests in the prelude to 5:19, when he urges the Ephesians not to be drunk with wine, but "filled with the Spirit" (5:18), which leads them to speak and sing to each other in the words of "psalms, hymns, and spiritual songs." Paul clearly implies that spiritual songs are characteristic of a spiritual life.

The early church took this to heart and clearly did not interpret Paul's injunction to mean that no new music in praise of God or Christ could be written or used in worship. An early collection of Christian hymns, generally called the "Odes of Solomon," dates from the first half of the second century, less than 100 years after Ephesians was written. Hymns were often used to preserve and teach doctrinal concepts or gospel stories as well as to praise God.

Music plays an integral role in Christian worship. Whether we sing psalms, traditional hymns, highly liturgical works, African-American spirituals, or more contemporary Christian music, our purpose is to encourage each other while offering praise to God—a combination that is hard to surpass.

Ephesians 6:10-20

ARMOR UP!

Finally, be strong in the Lord and in the strength of his power.
—Ephesians 6:10

What's your morning routine? All of us have some pattern, more or less organized, by which we get ourselves ready to face the day. We may put on an antiperspirant to guard against undue sweating, and brush our teeth to ward off cavities. We put on clothes to protect ourselves from the weather (and from embarrassment). We may eat a full breakfast or grab a quick snack to give us energy for the morning. One way or another, we prepare ourselves for what lies ahead.

How many of us give any thought to spiritual preparation? As Paul comes to the end of his letter, having offered both encouragement and instruction to the church, he closes with a fervent admonition for believers to prepare themselves daily for spiritual battle. "Finally," he says …

BE STRONG IN THE LORD
(v. 10)

"Be strong in the Lord," Paul says, "and in the strength of his power." All that follows in vv. 11-17 is an elaboration on this basic notion that the primary source of strength is the very one in whom we have entrusted our lives. ♻

All of us can name obstacles we must face each day, reasons we must be strong. We want to be strong for our children or for other family members who depend on us. We need strength to accomplish good work in our profession, whether it is homemaking or industry or management or public service or finding ways in retirement to contribute to the greater good. Sometimes we face so many physical or emotional demands that we hope and pray for

Strong three ways: Paul uses three different words to speak of strength or power. The word for "be strong" is the second-person plural imperative form of the verb 'endunamoō, which is formed from the prefix 'en- and a verbal form of the noun dunamis, from which we get English words such as "dynamic," "dynamo," and "dynamite." To be strong is to be empowered, and our greatest source of power is in God, whose Spirit indwells and empowers those who are openhearted enough to receive such gifts.

The extended phrase "in the strength of his power" employs two additional words for strength, power, or might. Kratos, the first, is often translated as "dominion." As participants in God's kingdom rule over all things, we can trust in God's power to make us strong. The second word is 'ischus, typically translated as "strength." We can have strength by trusting in God's power.

strength just to get through the day.

That's not what Paul has in mind, though. He's more concerned with our finding strength to overcome the influence of evil, the daily temptations we must face as we seek to follow Paul's previous pleas to walk worthily of our faith and to imitate Christ by loving others as Christ loved us.

For Reflection: *Have you ever employed a particular strategy to help you "be strong in the Lord"? Some people have memorized various scriptures and recite appropriate verses to encourage them in times of temptation or weakness. Others have worn WWJD ("What Would Jesus Do?") bracelets to remind themselves to ask that question when making decisions. Others may wear a cross around their neck or carry one in their pocket as a regular reminder to trust in Christ and remain strong in the face of trials. Have you tried these or other practical aids to promote spiritual strength?*

WEAR THE ARMOR OF GOD
(vv. 11-17)

Paul elaborates on his call to trust in God for strength by laying out a dire warning against evil influence, followed by an extended metaphor on the kind of "armor" that would befit soldiers in the kingdom of God.

Some readers take vv. 11-12 as a literal description of demonic beings that consciously seek, like the minion Screwtape in C. S. Lewis' *The Screwtape Letters*, to lead believers astray and engineer their downfall.

Paul rarely speaks of evil in embodied form, as do those who fear the influence of literal demons. More commonly, he refers to the influence of evil with words such as "the flesh," "the world," "this age," or "sin." The thought of evil beings with superhuman power was very much in vogue in Paul's day, however, and he adopted it in his letters. Whether Paul believed in a realm of insidious demons or simply adopted language that he knew would communicate to his readers, we can't be sure—but early writers such as Paul sought every means to get their message across.

Thus, Paul says that we do not struggle against flesh and blood alone, "but against the rulers, against the authorities, against the cosmic powers of this present darkness, against the spiritual forces of evil in the heavenly places" (v. 12). Some writers assert that terms such as "rulers," "authorities," and "powers" describe an array of supernatural beings who rebel against God, threaten humanity, and must be held at bay by angels and archangels in their own ranks. (See "The Hardest Question" on page 68 for more on this tricky subject.)

Paul writes as if he adopts this view of reality, and speaks in a way that he knows will resonate with his readers, but avoids undue speculation. For Paul, the important thing is that no evil power can stand against God in Christ, for God had raised Christ "far above all rule and authority and power and dominion, and above every name that is named, not only in this age but in the age to come" (1:21, see also Rom. 8:38-39).

God's invincible power is available, Paul believed, but not automatic. Believers must consciously put their trust in God and bedeck themselves with the protection God offers if they are to overcome evil. ♦

Paul describes this process through the overarching metaphor of putting on "the whole armor of God" (v. 13-17), which will enable the believer to "stand firm" against the power of evil.

♦ Paul's model? Writers often note that Paul, writing from prison, would have had daily exposure to Roman soldiers. When dressed in their full gear, such soldiers would have had more clothing and equipment than Paul describes, but he is not interested in an inventory of armor options: he uses only the metaphors that he needs to make his point.

Paul identifies six items that the well-equipped believer needs for spiritual warfare. The first is "the belt of truth" (v. 14a). This is reminiscent of Isa. 11:5, which speaks of the coming messiah as wearing a belt of righteousness and faithfulness. ♦

> **⊌ Where's the belt?** There
> is no word for "belt" in the text,
> but it is generally supplied by
> modern translations. The literal
> meaning is "wrap your waist
> with truth," which could imply
> something more than a belt.

Beneath their other armaments, as a first layer of protection, Roman soldiers wore a leather apron around their waist that was wide enough to protect the thighs. The first step in confronting evil is recognizing what is truth and what is a lie. Deception is a powerful weapon, but truth can defeat it.

The second piece of armor is "the breastplate of righteousness" (v. 14b), which calls to mind Isa. 59:17, a prophetic image of divine justice in which God "put on righteousness like a breastplate."

The image of righteousness is two-pronged. In one sense, any righteousness we have comes to us from God, but as redeemed sinners we are called to live a faithful and righteous life—the sort of life that does not make room for evil.

A soldier needs good footwear that will hold up for long marches or extended battle on rough terrain: lame fighters can hardly be effective. Roman soldiers wore high-top leather shoes such as heavy sandals, but with a thick sole. Paul's third admonition relates to the feet, but without using the word "shoes." Again, he draws from an image in Isaiah, who spoke of the beautiful feet of "those who bring good news, who proclaim peace." ⊌

> **⊌ Defense or offense?**
> Whether Paul has in mind that
> one is strengthened or prepared
> by the gospel of peace, or that
> one should go out to proclaim the
> good news of peace is not entirely
> clear. A literal translation would
> be something like "putting on the
> feet the preparation/readiness of
> the good news of peace" (v. 15).

The NRSV sees this as a call to proclaim the gospel ("as shoes for your feet put on whatever will make you ready to proclaim the gospel of peace"), but most modern translations see the gospel of peace as making one's feet ready for battle (e.g., "and with your feet fitted with readiness that comes from the gospel of peace," NIV). In other words, to stand against evil we must have our feet firmly planted in the gospel.

For Reflection: *In the 1994 movie* Forrest Gump, *Forrest observes "My momma always said you can tell a lot about a person by their shoes; where they go, where they've been . . ." What might your shoes—and the places they take you—say about you?*

The fourth item in the Christian's armor is "the shield of faith," which protects against the "flaming arrows" of evil (v. 16). Roman soldiers carried a large wooden shield about four feet tall and more than two feet wide. The shield was covered with leather that could be soaked with water to protect against arrows, even those that had been covered with pitch and set afire.

We are surrounded by harmful influences or pressures that would lead us astray, but holding on to faith in Christ enables us to deflect or extinguish verbal darts that would wound our spirits and damage our relationship with God.

Two last components of Paul's metaphorical spiritual armor are mentioned in v. 17: Believers are to complete their protective outfit by putting on "the helmet of salvation and the sword of the Spirit, which is the word of God." Isaiah 59:17 speaks of God wearing a helmet of salvation, but in this text, Paul sees God's gift of salvation as a helmet that gives the believer hope and confidence that God is with us and victory is sure.

Commentators often note that the sword is the believer's only offensive weapon, but a sword can serve a defensive purpose, as well. The kind of sword Paul commends finds its source in the Spirit and its effectiveness in "the word of God." This can be understood in a variety of ways, and is not limited to the Bible.

The Bible as we know it did not exist when Paul wrote these words: The rabbis hadn't even settled on what should be included in the Hebrew Bible until years after Paul's death, and the writings that would make up the New Testament had just begun to take shape. But Paul knew that divine inspiration could be found in those books that were accepted as scripture. When Jesus was tempted during his wilderness sojourn, he fended off each attack with a quotation from scripture (Matt. 4:1-11, Mark 1:12, Luke 4:1-13). Christians who read the Bible and seek a word from God may also find verses that express what they need to overcome temptation or doubt and stand strong.

> ⬥ **Tell me a story:** Seeking an imaginative way to interpret this text for the church, I once wrote a fictional story based on the text and used it as an extended introduction to a sermon. It was published as "Cloud Fights" in my book *Telling Stories: Tall Tales and Deep Truths.*[1]

But Paul also believed that God, through the Spirit, could give a needed word directly to believers who faced times of trial. Jesus assured his followers that they could be brave in the face of potential arrest, believing that the Spirit would tell them what they needed to say to their accusers (Matt. 10:19). ⬥

PRAY IN THE SPIRIT
(vv. 18-20)

Paul concludes his letter with an appeal to prayer that is so closely connected to the preceding verses that one might consider it to be the final element in the spiritual soldier's equipment: Soldiers do not fight alone, but at the direction of their commander, with whom they must communicate.

Having commended the sword of the Spirit, Paul immediately calls believers to "pray in the Spirit on all occasions with all kinds of prayers and requests" (v. 18). Followers of Jesus should adhere to his example of being steeped in prayer. Paul urges prayer for "the saints" (other Christians) and requests a special prayer for himself, that he will be given the words he needs to "fearlessly make known the mystery of the gospel" (v. 19) as an "ambassador in chains" (v. 20).

Note the similarity of this thought to the preceding idea that the sword of the Spirit provides needed words from God. Paul was a prisoner in chains, but he was neither defenseless nor without his sword. If Paul could live in such conditions and yet bravely proclaim the good news, perhaps he really does have something to teach us.

> **For Reflection**: *Do you find Paul's extended metaphor about "spiritual armor" to be helpful, or off-putting? Some readers have a hard time connecting with military metaphors. Imagine instead a firefighter's turnout gear, or software designed to protect your computer against viruses or malware. Could you turn one of these into an extended metaphor for guarding oneself against temptation, or come up with other metaphors that might speak more aptly to modern believers?*

THE HARDEST QUESTION

What about the "spiritual forces of evil in the heavenly places"?

Paul writes as if he believes in a host of spiritual powers that live and battle on some heavenly level between the divine and earthly realms. Should we adopt this view as our own understanding of reality?

The dualistic notion of good and evil forces battling it out in the heavens was unknown to the ancient Hebrews prior to the exile. Following Cyrus' defeat of the Babylonians in 538 BCE, the Persians dominated the Middle East for the next 200 years, and the Hebrews lived under their sway.

Although Cyrus, like other Persian leaders, was tolerant of other religions and even supported their practice, it was inevitable that the dominant Persian religion—Zoroastrianism—would influence popular thought.

Zoroastrianism was founded by Zoroaster (also known as Zarathustra), whose origin is uncertain but whose teaching might date back as far as the second millennium BCE. From around 650 BCE to 600 CE, Zoroastrianism was the official religion of Persia (modern Iran). Today it is one of the world's smallest religions: Less than 200,000 adherents still claim to be Zoroastrians, according to a 2006 report in the *New York Times.*

Zoroastrianism is monotheistic in that it envisions a high god (Ahura Mazda), but in practice it holds to a very dualistic notion of reality in which a good spirit called Spenta Mainyu fosters truth and goodness in the world, while the evil spirit Angra Mainyu opposes the truth and promotes evil.

Many scholars believe these Persian concepts contributed to the emergence of Satan in Judaism and early Christianity as a supernatural incarnation of evil who does battle with the angelic forces of God. In most of the Old Testament, the word "satan" is preceded by the definite article *ha,* meaning "the." Thus, *hasatan* means "the accuser"—only once, in 1 Chron. 21:1 (written late in Israel's history, after the exile), is Satan used as a personal name.

The latter half of the book of Daniel, the last Old Testament book written, doesn't speak of Satan, but imagines demonic powers leading supernatural armies of evil against angelic "princes" who command heavenly forces of good.

This dualistic imagery of competing heavenly powers continued to be a popular way of thinking in Paul's day, so it was natural that he would follow conventional notions of reality when writing.

This does not mean, however, that we need to live in fear of heavenly powers or that we should visualize demons flying around like invisible witches that would cause us harm if we do not pray for angels to protect us. This is the sort of image one finds in popular books by novelists such as Frank Peretti, whose imaginary tales of spiritual warfare have sold more than 15 million books, but they are just that—imaginary.

There's simply not enough evidence, biblical or otherwise, to assume that anyone can speak with authority about ranks of supernatural beings, whether good or evil. What we can be sure of is that evil exists, and that the human heart alone is quite capable of deep depravity without requiring demonic assistance. Whether we think of evil as internally generated or an amorphous supra-natural power or as inspired by demonic forces, Paul wants us to be equally confident that God, working in us through the Holy Spirit, can overcome whatever powers of evil there might be. We need not live in fear.

NOTE

[1]Tony Cartledge, *Telling Stories: Tall Tales and Deep Truths* (Macon, GA: Smyth & Helwys, 2008), 91-98.

AFTERWORD

S tudying the letter to the Ephesians can be an elevating experience. Paul (assuming he is the author) begins (1:1-14) by challenging readers to "look up" to Christ and celebrate the blessings Christ offers: redemption that leads to an internal inheritance as children of God, empowered by the Holy Spirit.

As people who were spiritually dead, we have the opportunity to "rise up" to a new life in Christ (2:1-10). This comes through the gift of God's grace in Christ and no work of our own, but that doesn't mean work is not in the picture. Paul insists that we are not saved *by* works, but *for* the good work God has called us to do.

As redeemed believers, we are part of a community of faith in which we can "huddle up" as an inclusive family or team to support each other in our common struggles and our mutual service to Christ (2:11-22).

In chapter 3, Paul exults in the amazing grace of God who not only brings us into relationship and gives us work to do, but also can "fill us up" through the Spirit to experience the presence of Christ, "who by the power at work within us is able to accomplish abundantly far more than all we can ask or imagine" (3:14-21).

We notice with chapter 4 that the tenor changes and Paul (or one of his disciples) charges the believers in Ephesus to "grow up" in unity and love as they live worthy of their calling, employing the various spiritual gifts with which they have been blessed (4:1-16).

To "build up" the community of faith, members must learn to speak the truth to each other, to manage their anger, and to treat others with kindness, always seeking to imitate Christ in their relationships both within the church fellowship and in the world at large (4:25-5:2).

Paul pleads with his readers—then and now—to "live up" to their calling by choosing wise paths, celebrating the Spirit's presence and trusting God to lead them in the right way as they practice mutual submission in their families and toward others (5:15-21).

Finally, Paul waxes metaphorical as he employs the image of a soldier's protective gear by encouraging readers to "armor up" with elements of truth, righteousness, peace, faith, salvation, and the Spirit of God (6:10-20).

As we read, as we study, as we live, may we trust Christ's Spirit to lead us onward and upward to become the people God has called us to be.

www.ingramcontent.com/pod-product-compliance
Lightning Source LLC
Chambersburg PA
CBHW060426090426
42734CB00011B/2469